◆ THAI ◆
TEXTILES

THAI TEXTILES

SUSAN CONWAY

THE BRITISH MUSEUM PRESS

© 1992 Susan Conway
Published by The British Museum Press
A division of The British Museum Company Ltd
46 Bloomsbury Street, London WC1B 3QQ

First published 1992
Reprinted 2001

British Library Cataloguing in Publication Data
Conway, Susan
Thai textiles.
I. Title
338.47677009593
ISBN 0-7141-2506-7

Designed by Harry Green
Set in Palatino by
Rowland Phototypesetting Limited
Bury St Edmunds, Suffolk
and printed in Spain by
Grafos S.A. Arte sobre papel

Cover Detail of a *pha prae wa,* Kalasin province.
The warp and weft are red silk with a
supplementary-weft pattern of diamonds and
flowers. (See also illustrations on pp. 6 and 161)

Page 1 Detail of a ceremonial banner, Khon Kaen
province, woven with a supplementary-weft
pattern of birds and elephants. (See also
illustration on p. 125.)

Pages 2-3 Enlarged detail of a cotton blanket
decorated with weft patterns in black cotton.
Isan Culture Museum,
Khon Kaen University. (See also p. 130.)

CONTENTS

The Lanna temple of Wat Phra Singh was constructed in 1345 in the city of Chiang Mai. The 18th-century mural paintings on the interior walls depict *jataka* stories. Scenes of everyday life include villagers wearing Lanna costumes and visitors from central Thailand in their traditional dress.

in paintings executed in a unique style, quite different from those I had previously seen in Bangkok. What was fascinating to me was the meticulous representation of costume and textiles. I had always admired Thai silk and cotton, and here were visual, historic records of a variety of costumes and weaving patterns which I had seen villagers wearing during the months spent sketching in the rice fields. What I had not realised was that these costumes were associated with a distinct northern Thai style portrayed in the mural paintings.

From the day of that first discovery I began to construct a photographic record of northern Thai temple mural paintings, with the help of my husband, Gordon Conway. The focus of the record was on the costumes and weaving patterns. In 1983 the study was enlarged to include north-east Thailand, the central plains and the main cities. What emerged was a revelation as each temple was a unique testimony to the range and vitality of the weaver's art. A photographic record was vital as there is so little written evidence of the history of textiles in Thailand and sadly no comprehensive collection such as might be housed in a national textile museum.

Village temples are graceful, elegant buildings: many are built of teak logged from the forests in the local hills; others are built of brick

ACKNOWLEDGEMENTS

My thanks go first to friends and colleagues who gave help and advice with the manuscript, particularly Marianne Straub, Jacqueline Herald, Deryn O'Connor and Amelia Uden. Thanks also go to Elizabeth Edwards and Kate White at the Pitt Rivers Museum, Oxford. At Khon Kaen University I am grateful to Acharn Suriya Smutkupt, Acharn Pairote Samosorn and Acharn Seurat who accompanied me on many field trips and shared so much of their knowledge. Thanks also go to Dr Terd Charoenwatana, Ian and Rattana Craig, Chainat Monaiyapong, and Dr Kanok and Dr Benjawan Rerkassem for help with research.

At Chiang Mai University Dean Nakhon na Lampang and his wife, Pornthip, made certain field trips especially interesting. My thanks go to Acharn Vithi Panichaphant who helped with the identification of textile patterns in the Chiang Mai valley and Ba Sangda Bansiddhi who gave me much useful information about vegetable dyes and traditional weaving patterns in north Thailand. Suwadee and Philip Salmon introduced me to the weavers of the Nan valley and kindly allowed me to photograph their textile collection. I am also grateful to Kun Akadej Nakbunlang, Kun Duangjith Thaveesri and Kun Patara Panichayakarn for allowing me to photograph their collections. In Bangkok I would like to thank M. L. Poomchai Chumbala for help with research on court textiles and allowing me to quote freely from his thesis, and Paothong Thongchua who allowed me to photograph some of his collection. Rosemary Wanchupela provided further information on vegetable dyes, and my friend Dr Gary Suwannarat gave advice, hospitality and constant encouragement.

In India Jasleen Dhamija provided information on trade with Thailand, and Usha Narayanan helped identify Burmese costumes in my mural photographs. Finally I would like to thank my husband Gordon who fell in love with Thailand long before I had been there, who introduced me to the country and its people, and took many of the photographs used in this book.

Detail of a Phu Tai *pha prae wa*, Kalasin province. The warp and weft are red silk with a supplementary-weft pattern of diamonds and flowers. (See also cover and illustration on p. 161.)

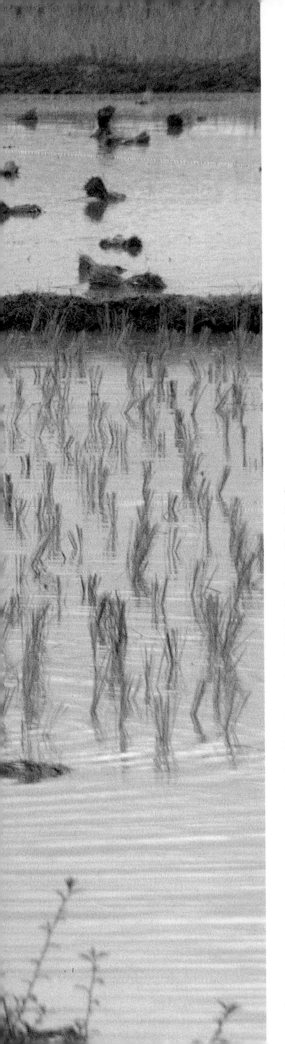

PREFACE

Thailand is a country with a rich cultural heritage, especially evident in its woven textiles. These range from cotton ceremonial banners to costumes of luxurious silks decorated with gold and silver thread. There is little published evidence of the role of textiles in Thai society, their ceremonial and social use, or of their importance to women who are the spinners, weavers and dyers. However, it is possible to assume that weaving is an ancient craft in Thailand because woven textiles are an integral part of the religious and social life of the Thai people. It is the purpose of this book to explain the integrated nature of textiles in rural and urban Thai society and their significance for women, and to draw attention to the superb quality of the weavers' and dyers' art.

The idea for this book developed in 1982 when I was working in Chiang Mai, north Thailand, preparing for an exhibition of my paintings and drawings inspired by the rice fields and rice culture. The exhibition opened at the British Council in Bangkok and toured Chiang Mai and Khon Kaen Universities. From the beginning of the planting season until after the rice harvest I spent many months sketching in the rice fields of the Chiang Mai valley. At the height of the monsoon season I was often forced to seek shelter from heavy rainfall, and one day when the rains were particularly heavy I found shelter in a small Buddhist temple at the edge of a village. When my eyes became accustomed to the dark interior I saw walls covered

A woman planting rice seedlings
in the Nan valley, north Thailand.

9

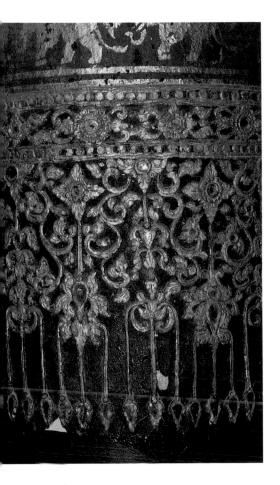

Gold-painted stucco inlaid with mirror glass, decorating a supporting pillar, from the interior of the 16th-century temple of Wat Phumin, Nan province. Similar pendant designs are seen in Thai textiles, especially in woven border patterns.

and stucco. Northern Thai temples have carved wooden eaves and pediments inlaid with mother-of-pearl; some are decorated with patterned stucco. Gold stencil patterns, which are also seen in the woven borders of many Thai textiles, and inlaid semi-precious stones decorate interior pillars, doors and walls. The temples also contain intricately carved wooden altarpieces and temple furniture, including pulpits and chairs for the senior monks.

The walls of the temples are decorated with scenes depicting the life of the Buddha and Buddhist cosmology. Painted in a dry fresco technique, they include representations of local architecture and village life, used as a backdrop to Buddhist religious stories. Court scenes show princes and princesses in brightly coloured costumes decorated with gold, often set in a background of pillows, curtains and wall-hangings, equally exotic in appearance. In village scenes local people are shown wearing woven ethnic costume, and invading armies, visiting foreigners and officials from Bangkok are also portrayed. In this pictorial manner the murals provide a unique insight into rural and urban life and also visual information about costume and textile patterns. By comparing the murals of central, north and north-east Thailand it is possible to identify many variations in weaving patterns and costume styles.

I had trained as a painter and had little technical knowledge of textile production, so in 1983 I returned to Britain to enrol on a postgraduate course in weaving and dyeing at Goldsmiths' College, London. Each summer I returned to Thailand to continue my research, interviewing weavers and dyers and photographing them at work. Where possible samples of costume and textiles were purchased or private collections photographed to add further information to the record. At the same time the photographing of mural paintings continued. The fieldwork was conducted throughout the valleys of north Thailand, from the Burmese border eastwards across the Chiang Mai valley to the Nan valley and south-east across the Korat plateau to the Mekong river, which forms the border with Laos. In Bangkok and Ayuthya I photographed Thai murals and examined textiles and costumes in private collections.

By 1986 I had acquired far more than just technical information about weaving and dyeing, and it became clear to me that textiles fulfil a more than decorative role in village society. The women of the villages explained the importance of textiles in all aspects of religious and social life. Textiles are interconnected with the seasonal cycle of rice cultivation, since women work in the fields during planting and harvesting and turn to cotton and silkworm rearing, spinning, weaving and dyeing during the rest of the year. These activities are the exclusive responsibility of women, and to my great pleasure village women sang lullabies for me and recited courtship poems in which beautiful girls are compared to fine silk.

They took me to their temples to see ceremonial banners woven for Buddhist festivals, and I joined in religious processions when textiles are presented to Buddhist monks.

However, I do not wish to give the impression that the stability of this ancient weaving culture will continue indefinitely. Tourism, Western methods of agriculture and the wholesale importation of foreign goods are bringing rapid change. Thai silk and cotton must now compete with factory produced textiles. Recently there has been a move to cash-crop silkworms, and imported species are replacing indigenous varieties thus threatening the integrated nature of traditional sericulture and the unique character of Thai silk.

The book begins with an ethnic and historic survey of the people of Thailand, including early migration patterns and the ascendance of the Tai, with emphasis on their religious traditions and social mores. There is a chapter describing weaving legends and the significance of textiles in religious and animist ceremonies. Chapter 5 examines the historic costume of Thailand, using evidence from ancient sculptures, Buddhist mural paintings, court records and early photographs. The book contains a detailed description of textile production from the cultivation of raw materials to weaving techniques. Regional variations in weaving patterns and their connection with ethnic identity are fully demonstrated in a range of woven textiles for dress, ceremonial occasions and for use by the householder.

The term Tai is used to describe an ethnic group made up of several sub-groups who inhabit Thailand, Burma, Laos, Vietnam and parts of eastern India and southern China. Before the nineteenth century the country which is now Thailand comprised separate kingdoms and principalities. At the end of the eighteenth century the northern kingdom of Lanna was united with the central kingdom. In 1893 the north-east region of Isan also became part of the kingdom, which was then known as Siam, with the capital in Bangkok. In 1939 the name was officially changed from Siam to Thailand. The term Thai is used to describe specifically the Tai of Thailand.

The text contains many Thai words which have been transcribed into the roman alphabet with the help of colleagues from the Universities of Khon Kaen and Chiang Mai. There are some words in north and north-east dialect which I have translated as accurately as I can. All Thai words in the text are explained in the Glossary.

19th-century mural painting, Wat Phumin, Nan province, depicting a group of young people in Lanna costume. The women wear horizontally striped ankle-length *phasin* and shoulder-sashes; their hair is secured in top knots decorated with gold, and they wear gold cylinders in their ears. The men, wearing patterned *pha chong kaben* and front-buttoned, mandarin-collared shirts, are tattooed from waist to knee. Their heads are shaved except for a circle of hair on top which is trimmed like a brush. They wear earrings resembling sprigs of flowers.

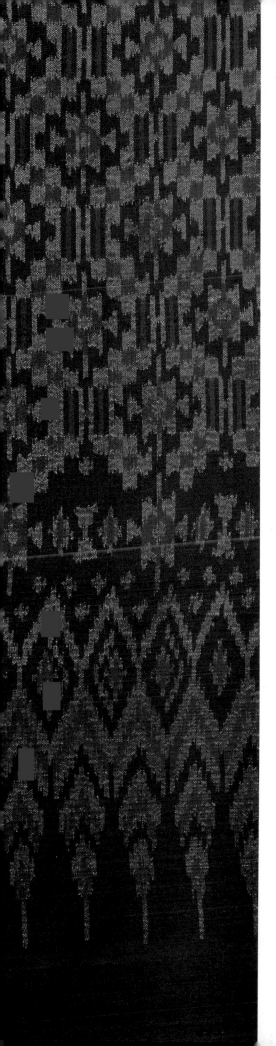

1

INTRODUCTION

THE PEOPLES OF THAILAND, THEIR HISTORY AND CULTURE

Thailand is a constitutional monarchy in South-East Asia lying between 5 and 21 degrees north of the Equator. Its total land area of 198,455 square miles (514,000 sq km) is bordered by Burma, Laos, Malaysia and Cambodia. The landscape includes tropical rain forest, rich alluvial plains, semi-arid plateau and deciduous tropical hill forests. About one-fifth of Thailand is forested, one-fifth covered by grass, shrub and swamp, and the remainder under settlement and cultivation. The climate is relatively constant throughout the year averaging 24–30°C (75–85°F), except in the highlands where the cool season in December may bring frost in the hills and cool, misty mornings in the valleys.

Prehistoric sites at Mae Hong Son province, north Thailand, and Ban Chiang in north-east Thailand indicate a long history of human settlement in the region (Pisit and Gorman 1976). Excavations in a cave near Mae Hong Son revealed stone adzes, pottery decorated with designs in soft clay and a small slate knife dating to 5,000 BC which was possibly used for harvesting wild rice. From about 1,500 BC an advanced culture based on rice-field cultivation using water-buffalo developed. Bronze jewellery, iron and bronze tools, painted pottery and glass beads, as well as traces of woven material imprinted on soil and on bronze and iron ornaments have been

Detail of a silk *phasin*, Khon Kaen province. Weft *matmi* patterns woven in plain weave. The dyes were produced from local plants and stick lac (shellac). The border pattern is similar to that seen in many Thai designs (see illustration on p. 11).

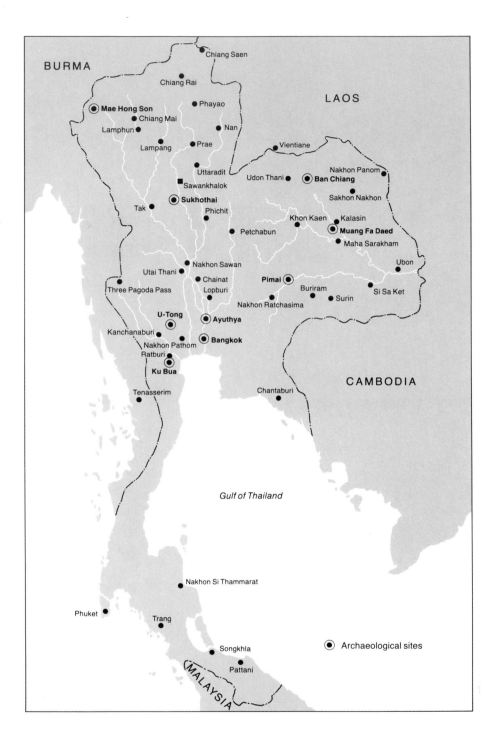

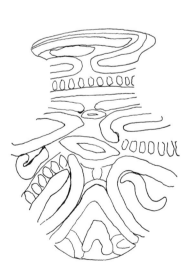

Drawing of a Bronze Age terracotta pot excavated at Ban Chiang. The painted designs resemble silkworms and silk cocoons.

excavated at the Ban Chiang site (Pisit and Diskul 1978). Of prime interest to the textile historian are the painted designs on Ban Chiang pottery which resemble silkworms, silk cocoons and mulberry leaves, suggesting an early silk-weaving culture.

The history of these metal-age people and their descendants is vague and confused. Old chronicles and legends mix myth and reality. Sometimes names of historical characters are quoted, often they appear to be transposed from the Buddhist folklore of India

16

and Sri Lanka or the folklore of southern China (Swearer 1974).
According to the historian Jean Boisselier contact between India and
Thailand first occurred in the third or fourth century AD. The arrival
of Indian influence meant adaptation of the already established
metal-age culture, the fusion of the two resulting in a Buddhist art
known as Dvaravarti.

The kingdom of Dvaravarti is thought to date from the sixth century and existed for between 500 and 600 years. The majority of the
people were Mon, an early Mongoloid people who originated in
western China. There were Lawa people of Austronesian origin and
a small number of Tais who migrated from southern China. At least
twenty Mon towns have been identified in Thailand extending from
the Menam Chao Phya river basin in central Thailand to Lamphun
in the north and Muang Fa Daed in the north-east. Mon cities were
fortified and surrounded by moats enclosed within earthen ram-
parts. Dams and irrigation channels were built, canals fed the water-
supply to the towns, and small ponds were dug to provide water for
Buddhist monasteries built outside the city walls. Most surviving
Dvaravarti architecture is Buddhist and consists of brick buildings
with laterite (baked clay) foundations (Pisit and Diskul 1978).

When Buddhism first reached Thailand is not accurately recorded,
but it is thought that the religion may have been introduced at the
time of King Asoka the Great of India, in approximately 300 BC (Pisit
and Diskul 1978). The silk route overland from India passed through
Burma to Yunnan, and Buddhist teachers travelling its route may
have made diversions to Thailand through Burma. Factual accounts
of conversion to Buddhism come from the second century AD when
Hinayana Buddhism reached central Thailand from southern India
and was adopted by the Mon people. According to the legendary
northern Thai chronicles the Mon Queen Camadevi introduced
Hinayana Buddhism to northern Thailand at the founding of the
city of Lamphun in the seventh century AD (Swearer 1974).

Mon towns proved to be a centre for art and culture, and according to legend Queen Camadevi of Lamphun also brought scholars,
jewellers, sculptors, silversmiths, goldsmiths and painters to live
and work in her kingdom (Swearer 1974). Although there are surviving examples of architecture, sculpture and jewellery from this
period, material related to textiles is confined to clay stamps possibly
used for imprinting simple geometric designs on cloth or on waist-
belts (van Esterik and Kress 1978). Terracotta and stone figurines
of Bodhisattvas (Buddhas-to-be) wearing ankle-length sarongs and
belts, imprinted with designs like those on the clay stamps, have
been excavated at U-Tong, central Thailand, one of the most important Dvaravarti towns (Pisit and Diskul 1978). The stucco and terracotta figures at Ku Bua, Ratburi province, also of the Dvaravarti
period, are portrayed wearing simple ankle-length skirts tucked at

Detail of a ceremonial cotton banner from San Pathong, Chiang Mai province. Plain cotton ground weave with a reddish-brown and black supplementary weft. The ship motif is also common in the ceremonial textiles of Sumatra.

the front and transparent, pleated sashes over the breasts. Jewellery includes elaborate necklaces and bracelets. Men wear sarongs with sash-belts and shoulder-sashes, and also wear earrings. The Lawa, who were a minority group in the Dvaravarti period, still live in small settlements in north Thailand and continue to weave simple cotton warp-ikat textiles, a technique which may pre-date the Dvaravarti period.

The link with Java and Sumatra

While the Mon towns flourished, further cultural exchanges occurred with a kingdom called Śrivijaya in the Indonesian archipelago. This kingdom established a vassal state in southern Thailand which thrived until the thirteenth century. Evidence for trade with Indonesia at this time includes ninth-century bronze sculptures excavated in southern Thailand which are similar to those found in central and eastern Java (National Museum, Bangkok). Evidence of textile exchange rests on the common design elements found in Indonesian and Tai woven textiles. Particularly interesting are the similarities between Sumatran and Tai Lue ceremonial banners which both contain woven images of ships with men aboard bearing banners or parasols of rank. Other shared imagery includes horses, serpents and birds which are woven in a representational way so that many species can be identified. Abstract designs include diamonds, hooks, interlocking scrolls and pendants which are woven as border decoration. Many Tai and Sumatran ceremonial textiles are oblong in shape, but the arrangement of the woven images dictate that the Tai are hung lengthways whereas the Sumatran ceremonial textiles are often displayed horizontally. Tai Lue ceremonial banners contain a supplementary weft of reddish-brown cotton on an undyed, hand-spun cotton ground weave, similar to those of Sumatra. Although these ceremonial textiles are woven primarily in cotton, there are also examples where silk and metallic threads were used by both Tai and Indonesian weavers.

The Khmer influence

From the seventh to the thirteenth centuries the Khmer kingdom to the east made a strong impact on Tai culture. Khmer temples have been excavated in north-east Thailand in the provinces of Surin, Nakhon Ratchasima and Buriram. The elaborately carved temple at Pimai, north-east Thailand, is contemporary with the twelfth-century temples of Angkor Wat, Cambodia. Chou Ta Kuan, Chinese envoy to the court at Sukhothai, central Thailand, recorded in the fourteenth century that the Khmers were taught to weave silk by the Tais and that the Khmers had no ancient tradition of silk weaving. Although the origins of silk weaving may be open to dispute, there is evidence of shared weaving patterns, notably ikat (*matmi*) where the designs are made by tie-dyeing the yarn before weaving. Historians have drawn attention to the similarity between *matmi* patterns and the decorative stone carvings of Angkor Wat (Sheares 1984). There are Khmer temples at Pimai with similar decorative carvings, and local weavers may have been influenced directly by these.

The ascendance of the Tai

Until the twelfth century the main inhabitants of north and north-east Thailand were Mon, Lawa and Khmer people, but in the thirteenth century the Tais began to play a prominent role in the history of the region. The Tai are believed to have come originally from Yunnan in southern China and slowly, over many centuries, moved south into Burma, North Vietnam and Laos, settling along the rivers and river valleys among the Khmer, Mon, Lawa and Burmese. By the thirteenth century the Tais had formed small independent city states ruled by Tai chieftains. These states formed alliances which challenged the dominance of the Mon and slowly diminished their power. One of the earliest Tai settlements in the north was established at Chiang Saen, on the banks of the Mekong river. A stone

Stone figure of a female divinity, Chiang Saen, 14th century. The folded, ankle-length skirt has carved floral patterns.

figure of a goddess from this period is dressed in an ankle-length skirt with carved floral patterns.

The Tai can be identified as an ethnic group on the basis of language and culture, including their distinctive textile patterns and costumes. They are lowland farmers, the majority living in rural communities and cultivating rice as their main crop, the women raising silk and cotton for yarn which they weave on frame looms. There are many groups and sub-groups occurring from Assam in the west to Vietnam and China in the east, and the textiles and costumes of the following groups are discussed. The first group are the Thai who are the Tai of Thailand and have been referred to in this way since the country was proclaimed Thailand in 1939. Before that date the central kingdom was called Siam, the northern kingdom Lanna and the north-east Isan. The Tai, whose ancestors were inhabitants of Lanna, are called Tai Yuan and are believed to be descendants of an even earlier northern kingdom called Yonok. The Tai Lue are descendants of the Tai of Sipsong Panna, southern China. Many were forcibly settled in the Nan valley and parts of Chiang Mai province, and they now form the majority group in Nan province. The Tai Lao come from the Mekong river region of Laos and are the majority group in north-east Thailand. The Lao ethnic sub-groups include the Lao Phu Tai, Tai Phuan and Lao Krang. The Tai Yai are the Tai from the Shan states of Burma who worked in northern Thailand, mainly in the timber trade.

The kingdom of Lanna, north Thailand

In the Thai language the word for a city state is *muang*, and the geographic extent of the Tai people can be studied by looking at a map of Thailand and picking out place names which include the words *meng*, *mong*, *muong* and *muang*. By the thirteenth century the Tai were a powerful people, led in the north by King Mengrai who controlled Chiang Mai, Chiang Rai, Chiang Saen, Lamphun and Lampang. By the fifteenth century the kingdom extended to include Prae, Nan and Phayao. It is from this time that the Lanna kingdom of north Thailand existed as an individual political and cultural state. A distinctive style of architecture, painting and the decorative arts, including textiles, developed. The Lanna kingdom was independent, although throughout its existence it was subject to incursions from Burma, and its borders with the central kingdom, Ayuthya, were from time to time disputed. In 1782 King Rama I moved his capital from Ayuthya to Bangkok and united Lanna with the central kingdom of Siam.

After unification Lanna retained a large degree of independence. Apart from visits to Bangkok to pay tribute in silver and gold, the princes of Lanna were left alone to rule as virtually free states. It was not until 1877 that a resident Siamese High Commissioner was

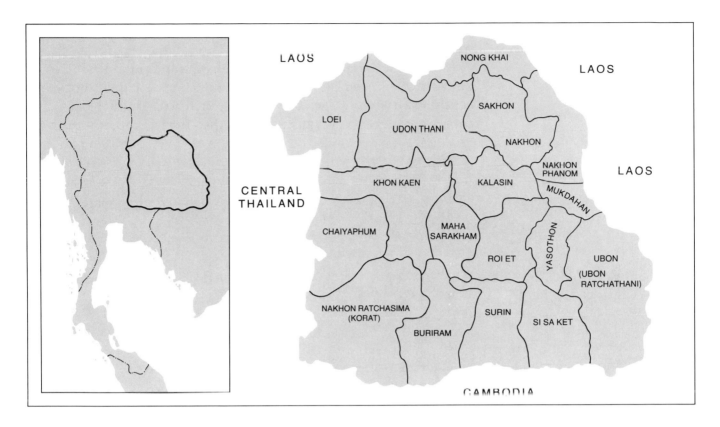

The provinces of Isan (north-east Thailand).

appointed at Chiang Mai (Le May 1926). His appointment and posting to the north with his staff brought Siamese fashion to the attention of the people of Chiang Mai. These new fashions are recorded in the Chiang Mai temple mural paintings and photographs of the period; but they did not extend far beyond the cities of Lanna, so that in the rural areas weavers continued to produce their own highly individualistic patterns and to wear ethnic costume until well into the twentieth century.

The region of Isan, north-east Thailand

The north-east region of Thailand known as Isan extends eastwards from the central plains to the Mekong river and south across the Korat plateau to the border with Cambodia. Isan was never an independent kingdom but an outlaying region which until the twentieth century was claimed at various times by Cambodia, Laos, central Thailand and Burma (Keyes 1967). The inhabitants of Isan are mainly of Tai Lao extraction. From the fourteenth century they migrated south from Yunnan, China. Migration to Isan from Laos was extensive from the beginning of the eighteenth century when 3,000 Tao Lao led by a Buddhist monk, Phrakhue Phon Samet, fled from the kingdom of Vientiane and settled in Isan. In 1793 further immigrants led by a Lao nobleman settled in an area which is now called Kalasin. Four years later further settlement took place in Khon Kaen. By the end of the eighteenth century Suwannaphum, Kalasin and Roi Et also contained Lao settlements (Keyes 1967). Further Tai Lao settlements took place on the Korat plateau and in the province of Maha Sarakham. The relationship with Bangkok was tenuous: Isan princes paid tribute in silver and gold and were occasionally required to send labourers to the capital. In the nineteenth century Siam was pressed between the rival expansionist tendencies of Britain in

A group of ladies from rural Thailand waiting to welcome King Rama V (King Chulalongkorn), *c.* 1900. They wear traditional woven *phasin* skirts and white sashes. Siam Society.

Burma and France in Laos. In 1893 a treaty between Siam and France recognised Laos as a French protectorate. The Siamese withdrew from the right bank of the Mekong river, and under the conditions of the new treaty Isan became a permanent part of the kingdom of Siam. Rama V then set about reforming the administrative system in Isan, creating provinces with governors and officials at district level to administer the region.

The presence of a large Tai Lao population has meant that many weaving patterns and costumes of the people of Isan have their origins in Laos. However, in southern Isan there is a population of

Temple mural painting of a
court scene, Wat Nong Bua,
Nan province.

about half a million Khmers who migrated from Cambodia and
settled mainly in the provinces of Surin, Si Sa Ket and Buriram.
They brought with them the traditional weaving patterns of the
Khmer, which add to the richness and variety of the textiles produced in Isan.

Cultural exchanges between Lanna, Isan and Ayuthya
From the mid-fourteenth to the sixteenth centuries there were diplomatic and cultural exchanges between Ayuthya, the Lanna kingdom
and the region of Isan. The Laotian kingdom of Lan Chang ('country

of a million elephants') with its capital in Vientiane included northern Isan in its territory. Laotian princes from Lan Chang married Lanna princesses, and a Laotian prince once claimed the throne of Lanna. There were treaties and marriage alliances made between the royal families of Laos and Ayuthya; King Chaiyachetsada Thirat of Laos assisted his brother-in-law, King Maha Chakaphat of Ayuthya, during war with Burma. Cultural links between Laos and Lanna can be seen in the similarity between Lanna script and the script used in the religious texts of Laos. There are examples of Buddhist temples in Isan which reflect a Lanna-Lan Chang style, for example at Monthon Udon, north-east Thailand (Samosorn 1989).

Although there is no written evidence, it is probable that during the marriage alliances arranged between Ayuthya, Lan Chang and Lanna, woven textiles were included in the dowries of the princesses. In this way court weavers were exposed to new patterns and costume styles. Whether this outside influence reached village weavers can only be a matter for speculation. The wearing of Isan and Lanna textiles at the court of Bangkok is well recorded. Princesses from north and north-east Thailand who married into the Bangkok royal family continued to wear their traditional costumes and regularly ordered woven fabrics from their home provinces (Chumbala 1985).

The kingdom of Sukhothai

Throughout the thirteenth century the Tai had continued to move south on to the central plains, where they began to dominate the empires of the Mon and Khmer, and in AD 1238 they expelled the Khmer from Sukhothai. Sukhothai in the thirteenth century was only a small kingdom but was situated on fertile land. Inscriptions of the time relate 'This Muang Sukhothai is good. In the water there are fish, in the fields there is rice . . . whoever wants to trade in elephants so trades. Whoever wants to trade in horses so trades. Whoever wants to trade in silver and gold so trades . . .' (Griswold and Prasert na Nagara 1967).

The most famous Tai ruler of Sukhothai was Ramkamhaeng, who by the beginning of the fourteenth century had increased the size of the kingdom across the central plains to Luang Prabang in the east and to the southern peninsula. In order to protect their borders from invasion King Ramkamhaeng and the northern princes of Chiang Mai and Phayao formed an alliance which resulted in a period of stability and expansion. The Sukhothai period is seen as the first great flowering of Thai art, and the restored monuments at Sukhothai today are a living reminder of this great culture. Ramkamhaeng established diplomatic relations with China, and Chinese craftsmen were invited to Sukhothai. In return Sukhothai sent regular diplomatic missions to China, returning with trade goods,

Princess Poonpisamai, daughter of Prince Damrong Diskul, dressed in Sukhothai style. Bangkok, c. 1900. Siam Society.

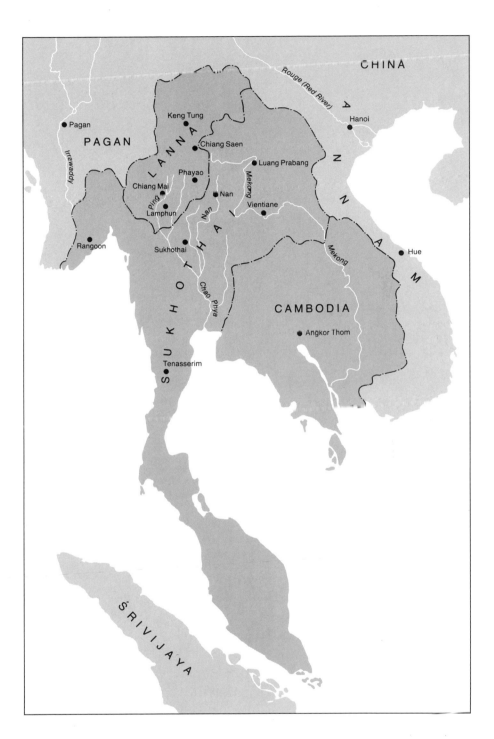

The kingdoms of Lanna, Sukhothai and Cambodia, late 13th-early 14th centuries.

including textiles. From the letters of Chinese diplomats in the thirteenth and fourteenth centuries we know that the most sought-after fabrics in Sukhothai were silk, velvet, satin and cotton. Some fabrics came from China, Burma and India, although cotton and silk were also woven locally. For ceremonial occasions the cotton was dyed in five colours – black, white, red, green and yellow – and was known as *bencharongse* (Chumbala 1985). Stone inscriptions at Sukhothai record the wearing of this five-coloured cloth and its use on

A row of bell-shaped stupas, Ayuthya, 15th century.

ceremonial occasions. In 1361 an important religious leader visited Sukhothai and by royal decree the five-coloured cloth was used to cover his path (Division of Education, 1964).

Sukhothai remained a wealthy and powerful kingdom throughout the reign of King Ramkamhaeng, but after his death in 1317 power diminished and in 1378 King Rama Thibodi annexed Sukhothai as part of his kingdom of Ayuthya, situated further south on the banks of the Chao Phya river.

The kingdom of Ayuthya

During the Ayuthya period (1350–1767) the Tai retained certain Khmer cultural traditions, including the presence of Brahmins and

INTRODUCTION

Buddhist monks at state ceremonies, a custom which continues in Thailand to this day. Ayuthya's monarchs took the title 'Lords of Life' reflecting the Khmer concept of a god king. As Ayuthya rose in power the life-style of the court became lavish, and court costumes of gold and silver brocade and jewel-embroidered silks reflected the power of the monarchy.

From the middle of the fifteenth century Muslim traders carried Indian textiles from the Coromandel coast to ports on the main trade routes in Sumatra, Java and Burma, from where they were dispatched to Ayuthya. At the end of the fifteenth century the Portuguese took over this trade, followed in the seventeenth century by the Dutch and the English (Irwin and Schwartz 1966). In the seventeenth century goods travelled between Europe, the Middle East, India, the East Indies, China and Japan. Trade goods shipped from Madras to Ayuthya travelled via the Straits of Malacca up the eastern coast of the Malay peninsula to the mouth of the Chao Phya

Above right Temple mural painting, Wat Phra Singh, Chiang Mai province, depicting the 19th-century palace of the governor of Chiang Mai with ladies peeping from the window. The curtains are imported, printed cottons of European or Indian origin.

river, known as the Bar of Siam. Ayuthya was 50 miles (80 km) up river and the total sailing time from Madras was about six months. An alternative route was to sail across the Bay of Bengal to Mergui, by river boat to Tenasserim, where middle men transferred the cargoes to small boats or to mules and elephants for the journey northeast to Ayuthya. Printed and painted cotton textiles were imported to Ayuthya from Surat and the Coromandel coast. These textiles were used as wall-hangings, room-dividers, floor-spreads and clothing (Gittinger 1982). They were hand-painted or printed with wooden blocks using a range of direct and resist-dye techniques. Accounts of this trade can be found in the records of the Dutch and English trading companies of the seventeenth century: 'Four Indian

Detail of a painted and printed cotton textile produced in India for the Thai market, 18th or 19th century.

ships, the last of the convoy from Masuleepatum have arrived, carrying all kinds of painted fabrics to raise some excitement in the cloth market, but most of the textiles will be sold directly to the Crown for it usually offers the highest prizes . . .' (Satkul 1970).

Indian *patolas* (double-ikat) textiles were also exported to Thailand. They are mentioned in accounts written by Europeans working in Asia. In the seventeenth century the French traveller Tavernier wrote: 'Patolas, which are the stuffs of silk, very soft, decorated all over with flowers of different colours, are manufactured at Ahmedabad. This is one of the profitable investments of the Dutch who do not permit any member of their company to engage in this private trade. They are exported to the Philippines, Borneo, Java, Sumatra and other neighbouring countries.'

Patola textiles are rectangular in shape and there are twelve basic designs. The central field contains patterns of plant and zoomorphic origin. The selvages are bordered by stripes or simple geometric patterns. The end borders contain floral, plant or animal motifs, geometric patterns and rows of zigzags and stripes. The court textiles of Thailand and Cambodia were influenced by the style of

Pages 32–3 Temple mural painting, Wat Phra Singh, Chiang Mai province, showing visiting Burmese dignitaries wearing a type of *lungyi*, called *paso*. The material, which is 10 yds (9 m) long, is passed around the waist and between the legs from front to back, then across the torso and over one shoulder. The patterns are *luntaya*, a tapestry-weave technique producing wavy-line designs. The officials wear round-necked shirts and loose jackets and the headgear of Burmese court officials. Tattoo patterns are visible just above their knees. The man leading the group is in rural costume.

patola, but weaving patterns of Siamese and Khmer origin were often substituted for Indian patterns. *Patola* textiles were worn as *pha chong kaben*, the material being wrapped and tucked around the body to create a pantaloon-style garment.

European textiles became fashionable during the reign of King Narai (1656–88). When the French arrived in Ayuthya they established excellent diplomatic relations with the court, and King Narai and Louis XIV exchanged letters. In 1684 diplomats arrived at the court of Versailles where Louis XIV declared that 'he was delighted to meet them and promised to help the King of Siam, his brother in anyway that he could' (Launey 1920).

Reports of French fashion reached King Narai, who according to the letters of the Jesuit Père Tachard, ordered the following items from Paris (Chumbala 1985).

1. A red velvet coat, embroidered in gold, decorated with pearls.
2. Two sleeveless cloaks made from red velvet, decorated with pearls, both have velvet trimmings, silk and gold lace decorations.
3. White velvet.
4. Blue velvet, red velvet trimmings embroidered in silk, gold lace, golden silk and pearls.
5. A scarlet cloak in the French style with Thai shaped sleeves.
6. Three pieces of cloth embroidered with silk and gold membrane to follow the patterns sent from Ayuthya.
7. Lace made to Thai designs.
8. Table cloths from Flanders.
9. An assortment of fine silks with gold floral patterns.
10. Striped fabric.

By the seventeenth century Ayuthya was a major centre for trade, with at least four textile markets where foreign merchants gathered to buy and sell. Records indicate that the citizens of Ayuthya were avid customers for Chinese silk, painted and printed cotton and brocaded silk from India, and European linen and lace (Chumbala 1985). Imported textiles were also used for interiors at court. In 1753 Sri Lankan diplomats described the reception rooms of the Royal Palace at Ayuthya as being full of expensive carpets and white linen.

The golden age of Ayuthya was to come to an abrupt end in 1767 when an invading Burmese army killed, looted and burnt the city to the ground. They took the royal family and thousands of citizens as hostages. A young general, Phya Tak Sin, escaped during the final seige of Ayuthya and regrouped with his men at Chantaburi on the Gulf of Siam from where they were able to expel the Burmese.

King Mongkut (Rama IV) and his consort, 1862. The king wears a *pha chong kaben* and jacket trimmed with gold. His consort wears a silk *matmi* patterned skirt and brocaded silk sash. Pitt Rivers Museum.

Khunying Sangad Wichayen, wife of a senior official in Bangkok, *c.* 1900. She wears a Western-style blouse trimmed with lace and a woven silk *pha chong kaben*. Siam Society.

With the city in ruins, Phya Tak Sin decided to build a new capital to the south at the site of a small fishing village at Thonburi. During his rule the Burmese made several further attempts to invade which he managed to repulse. The atmosphere of the time meant that the elaborate costumes worn during the Ayuthya period were replaced with simpler styles of dress. Women had to be ready to fight side by side with their men and wore simple *pha chong kaben* and cut their hair short to disguise themselves as men and lessen the threat of sexual assault from invading soldiers (Na Nakorn 1979). In 1782 King Rama I of the Chakri dynasty replaced Tak Sin as ruler, moving the capital across the river to Bangkok, and there followed a period of expansion when new palaces and temples were built.

The court of Bangkok

During the nineteenth century the kingdom of Siam flourished. Arts and culture were encouraged by the royal family, diplomatic relations were established with the West, and schools, hospitals and roads were built. Peace brought stability to the Tai who prospered in the river valleys and towns which in previous times had been devastated by incursions from Burma. Fashions in Bangkok reflected this new period of stability which followed the chaos and disruption caused by war with Burma. The people had given up the codes of dress established during the Ayuthya period, and from his new court in Bangkok Rama I introduced new rules which were combined with contemporary Siamese taste. High-ranking officials were permitted to wear brocaded silks and carry yellow silk umbrellas. Those of lower status were required to wear simpler fabrics and carry plain umbrellas. Goldsmiths and jewellers were instructed to sell lavish gold and diamonds only to those of high rank (Chumbala 1985).

By the middle of the nineteenth century European fashions were becoming popular among the élite, although they were adapted to suit local taste. Women wore traditional *phasin* skirts or *pha chong kaben* wraps with European-style blouses, Western silk stockings and shoes. They wore a sash over the blouse, woven of local silk or imported silk chiffon. Lacy blouses with bows and Western-style hats also became fashionable, and camisole tops and ornate puff-sleeved jackets were popular with the young. This blending of Siamese and Western fashions was to continue into the twentieth century, although traditional dress was still worn for ceremonial and state occasions.

During the nineteenth and early twentieth centuries Lanna and Isan remained outposts of the kingdom, journeys from Bangkok took many days by boat, horse, mule or elephant, and parts of the route were impassable during the rainy season. As a result of this relative isolation the individual cultures of Lanna and Isan

Temple mural painting, Wat Phumin, Nan province, depicting Europeans and Asians in 19th-century costume. Western traders and Christian missionaries arrived in northern Thailand in the mid-19th century.

flourished into the twentieth century. There was formal contact from the nineteenth century between the main towns of Lanna and Isan and Bangkok through government officials who were sent to administer the regions. Foreign traders and missionaries also worked in the towns and villages (Hudson 1965). Some of these foreign visitors are vividly portrayed in the Buddhist temple mural paintings of Lanna.

In early photographs taken in Chiang Mai around 1890 some Siamese administrators and professionals sent from Bangkok wear a mixture of Siamese and Western dress. Female members of the royal family of Chiang Mai are occasionally photographed in Edwardian blouses worn with *phasin* skirts, but in the countryside villagers are photographed wearing their regional costumes.

Khon Kaen and other main towns of Isan were also administered by officials from Bangkok, but trade with Isan did not match that of prosperous Lanna with its teak forests and fertile agricultural land. However, Isan produced the finest silk which was purchased by the royal families of Chiang Mai, Nan and Bangkok and was worn by the wealthy. The rural areas of Lanna and Isan were little affected by foreign trade and commerce in the towns. These communities continued with village traditions of Buddhism and the seasonal production of rice.

The rice cycle

Farmers in Thailand live in village communities and grow glutinous (sticky) rice as their staple food. There is an old saying in Thailand that every free man has the right to cultivate up to twenty-five *rai* (about 10 acres or 4 ha) to support his family. Today Thailand remains primarily a nation of small farmers occupying the valleys and plains and sometimes described as 'The people who live within the sound of a frog'. Rice has special significance in Thai culture and is associated with Buddhism in village mythology as this quotation illustrates: 'Rice is both excellent and costly. Lord Buddha and rice were born at the same time. Rice came along with religion. The teacher has given praise in verses, saying that through the possession of rice can be obtained transcendent virtue' (from 'The Myth of the Rice Spirit', Tambiah 1970).

The rice cycle begins when the monsoon rains arrive (usually in June), and fields are ploughed by water-buffalo. Rice seedlings are tended first in a rice nursery at the edge of the field where they can be watched carefully and are then transplanted into irrigated fields at the wettest time of the year. When working in the fields farmers lunch on glutinous rice prepared at home in the early morning and carried to the fields in rattan baskets. The cooking of glutinous rice involves a wooden steamer set over a cauldron of boiling water. At lunch time the rice is removed by hand from the basket, rolled in the fingers and dipped into dishes which may consist of a curry or a little fish caught in the water of the fields. Special field shelters provide shade at mealtimes. Some are interesting examples of small-scale village architecture, built of bamboo and wood with recent additional materials such as corrugated iron and plastic. Locally woven rush mats cover the floors. The patterns woven on rice baskets and floor mats are similar to those seen in some woven Thai textiles.

Rice is harvested in the dry season (January and February) when families gather together working from field to field. They cut the

Temple mural painting, Wat Buak Khrok Luang, Chiang Mai province. The women wear simple, horizontally striped *phasin*, with their hair in top knots. One woman is stirring a wooden pail of glutinous (sticky) rice which is steaming over an earthenware pot.

Aerial view of the Chiang Mai valley, which in the rainy season is planted with sticky rice. Complex irrigation systems have existed in the valley since the 13th century.

Pages 38–9 A valley near Mae Hong Son, north Thailand. Rice grain is being winnowed into a large woven basket. One man tosses the grain into the air with a long-handled shovel; the other two wave round bamboo fans above the falling grain to disperse the chaff.

stalks with a small sickle, then thresh and winnow by hand. The most picturesque method for threshing grain involves the use of large woven baskets each over 6 ft (2 m) in diameter. The sheaves are tapped against the side of the basket and the grain drops inside. The baskets are carried from field to field so that harvested plants do not have to be moved. The grain is then put into sacks, loaded on to fretworked wooden carts drawn by oxen or buffalo and driven back to the village. In north Thailand the sun sets early at harvest time, the nights are cool and in some fields farmers have begun to burn the rice stubble. When the rice crop is safely stored in the family rice barn next to the house, then hard field labour is over until the next planting season. Women can now turn to the cotton bolls and silkworms which they have cultivated in readiness for spinning and weaving after the rice harvest.

In the valleys where the land is fertile and irrigated this yearly pattern of the rice cycle has continued over many centuries. But in areas of north-east Thailand where the soil is poor and the monsoon rains irregular many farmers and unmarried girls become part of the migratory labour force to the cities. Where possible, married women with young children and the elderly stay in the villages, providing some stability in the community. In villages where the rice crop is insufficient to feed the family weaving of silk and cotton textiles for sale makes a vital contribution to the family income and helps prevent further migration to the cities. If the rice crop occasionally fails, women may use textiles as a bank, selling pieces only in bad years. Textiles can make an important contribution to the village economy, but as explained in Chapter 2 they also play an important role in the religious and social life of the village.

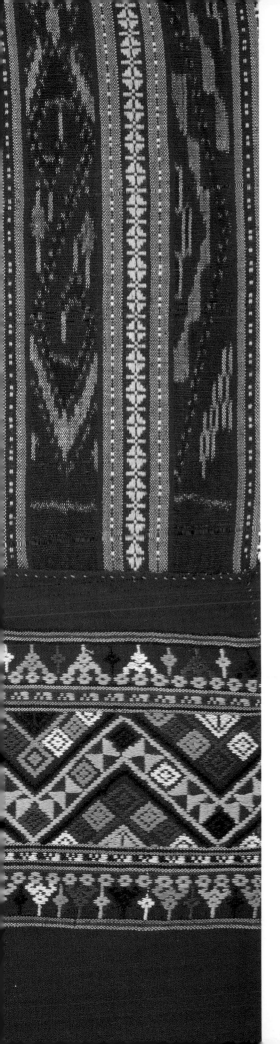

2

❖

TEXTILES,
RELIGION AND
SOCIETY

Textiles, whether worn, presented as gifts, or displayed in religious ceremonies, accompany men and women throughout their lives, marking the passage from birth to death and the passing seasons, reflected in the major Buddhist festivals. Life begins with brightly patterned costumes, grandmothers progress to fine muted tones, and the elderly wear dark sombre hues. Unwoven yarn has symbolic uses: cotton fibres are hand-spun, rubbed with beeswax and blessed by the monks before being used as a symbolic enclosure for worshippers during religious ceremonies. The yarn is also used as a symbol of binding body and spirit together (see pp. 48, 54).

Unlike many other parts of the world weaving among the Tai is exclusively a female skill, yet according to an ancient Tai legend the guardian spirits taught women to weave through a male intermediary, Khun Borom. The ancestry of Khun Borom has been subject to continuing speculation: in some Tai legends he is described as a king of Yunnan, southern China; in others he is hailed as a legendary ancestor of the Tai Lao. Khun Borom acted as intermediary for the Tai guardian spirits when they laid the foundations of Tai culture. He is credited with power to make the land fertile by bringing seasonal monsoon rains. He taught farming skills and all Tai arts

Detail of a *phasin*, Phichit province. The design contains rows of silk weft *matmi* alternating with bands of cotton containing supplementary-weft patterns. The hem has a red cotton ground weave brocaded with geometric motifs.

41

Temple mural painting, Wat Phumin, Nan province, depicting a Lanna lady selecting spools of yarn while working at a Thai frame loom. There are four heddle shafts with bamboo foot pedals and a carved wooden beater. The warp passes up over the top beam and is secured on the beam above the weaver's head.

and crafts. With guidance from the guardian spirits he gave women the skills of sericulture, cotton cultivation, spinning, weaving and dyeing. Khun Borom designed weaving equipment, the loom, spindles, needles and shuttles. He declared that weaving was a household duty to be carried out with skill and diligence, to bring respect in this life and spiritual merit to be rewarded in the next.

The legends of Khun Borom survive in the form of homilies which are recited in the villages of north-east Thailand. The following are extracts from a collection of Isan homilies translated from local dialect into central Thai by Acharn Jeruwan Thamawat (translation into English provided by Acharn Seurat, Khon Kaen University).

> A good wife is like a ploughshare. If she is skilled at weaving, then her husband can wear fine clothes. A wife who talks harshly and is unskilled at her loom makes a family poor and shabby in dress.

> Don't hurriedly sell your cloth, keep it until the time is right and you can ask a good price. Measure your newly woven cloth with skill. Show it to an expert and if she approves, keep the cloth until you can get a fair price.

> If you want to be rich, you must be creative and diligent. Be careful in making merit and give donations to the monastery. Be skilled at the loom and you will be respected and never get into debt.

42

Right A young girl weaving in the area under the house, Ban Don Chai, Nan province.

Above A village carpenter carving wooden shuttles, Ban Don Chai, Nan province.

A cotton sampler of *khit* patterns, Ban Nong Hang, Kalasin province. Smithsonian Institution, Washington, DC (photographer Victor Krantz).

In the rural areas of Thailand all women are traditionally taught to weave, and weaving is seen as a manifestation of womanhood. Men make the equipment for textile production, including looms, shuttles and spinning-wheels, but they do not touch the loom once it is set up and in use (verbal communication with Acharn Suriya Smutkupt). An exception is made for male transvestites who are accepted as weavers in village society.

The relationship between weaving and success as a wife and householder is clearly recognised in traditional village society where young women known to be skilled weavers are prized as future brides. Girls are taught to weave by their mothers or female relatives and from early childhood watch the many processes of cultivation, spinning, weaving and dyeing taking place at home and around the village. Patterns for weaving are not written down but passed on by example from one generation to the next. If the pattern is complex, then samplers may be kept as a reference. After a childhood spent watching the adults, and increasing her skills during adolescence, by the time she marries a girl will know how to weave a variety of textiles for use at home and for ceremonial occasions.

Courtship and engagement
The traditional season for courtship is after the rice harvest when women spend time spinning and weaving in the courtyards of their

43

homes. In the evenings, by lamplight, the young men gather to watch and court the unattached girls. In many villages in north-east Thailand old ladies will recall the weaving seasons in their youth, when visiting suitors brought musical instruments to serenade them as they worked. In north-east Thailand *payar* (courtship prose) uses weaving terms as metaphors for physical and romantic love (Thamawat 1980, translated by Acharn Seurat, Khon Kaen University):

Temple mural painting of Burmese lovers, Wat Phumin, Nan province. She wears a loose-fitting jacket and bustier, with gold cylinder earrings. He wears a twisted and knotted headcloth, worn in Burmese style. The large hole in his earlobe is devoid of decoration. The Burmese are often portrayed in northern Thai mural paintings, either as soldiers, visiting dignitaries or labourers.

Boy: Let me sit, sister. You are as beautiful as a morning star. Let me sit beside you who look like a goddess from Heaven.

Girl: Sit down, please, sit down. Nobody occupies the place here beside me, but don't stand by the porch – it is a place for the dog.

Boy: You are to be compared to the finest silk cloth and the most delicate silk thread. You are as cool and beautiful as silk. You beat cloth with the finest teeth beater to make the finest silk cloth. You are a twenty-five-teeth beater.

Girl: Oh, brother, if I am compared to the twenty-five-teeth beater, then I must search for the finest thread to put in my loom.

Boy: I am to be compared to an old shawl that you will throw away so that you can acquire a new one. You are a good beater of cloth, a fifty-five-teeth beater. I wish I had thread for

44

you to weave, but I do not know if you are interested in me or if you think I am an undyed inferior yarn. Please do not think of me in that way but put my thread into your loom.

Girl: You must never compare me with cotton but only with fine silk.*

Boy: I have decided to carry an axe and cut wood for a fire. I will catch fish in the traps and return with them in a basket. I long to wear silk cloth so I will help raise silkworms and bring mulberry leaves to feed them. I will carry the rice seedlings for you from the nursery and help you to transplant them in the fields.

* The comparison of fine silk with a girl's beauty is a popular simile in courtship prose. Silk is often used to describe women of delicate beauty, cotton representing those with coarser features. In some prose lines men are compared with the outer rough filaments of the silk cocoon and women with the fine, smooth, inner strands.

A girl who is charmed by a suitor (perhaps attracted by his courtship prose) may become engaged, although this may also depend on family approval. Traditionally a young man is considered ready for marriage after he has finished his term as a novice monk. Before his novitiate he is described as 'not ripe' or 'not cooked' (verbal communication with Acharn Suriya Smutkupt). The marriage age for girls is flexible, but to be eligible a girl should also be considered mature. One measure of this is her ability to weave a variety of textiles including a traditional *phasin* (skirt), *pha sabai* (sash), *pha hom* (blanket), *pha lop* (sheet), *maun* (pillow) and *pha sarong* (sarong). In some regions the ultimate challenge to a young girl's skill is to weave an elaborate *teen jok*, a decorated hem border for a *phasin*, which may take up to six weeks to complete.

When an engagement is announced and if the families can afford it, an astrologer will be consulted to set an auspicious day and time for the wedding. The future bride then becomes very busy weaving textiles for her new home and those she will present to her family and future in-laws. The customary gifts presented at times of marriage vary, but a bride may present a *phasin* to her mother-in-law and will decide with her own mother who else should receive gifts. Recipients are relatives and friends of the bride and groom and they, in exchange, give a wedding present, often money, gold if they are wealthy. In Thailand gift customs at the time of marriage vary according to the ethnic background of the family. In the Nan valley a Tai Lue bride weaves the *phasin* she will wear on her wedding day and a sheet for her marriage bed, richly decorated with supplementary-weft patterns. She weaves an indigo shirt and trousers for the groom to wear at work in the fields. At Ban Don Chai, Nan province, the bride also weaves mosquito nets and a

Detail of a cotton bed sheet, Nan province. Plain hand-spun cotton warp and weft with a supplementary-weft pattern of hooks, zigzags and flowers, woven in red and black cotton and lilac, yellow, green and brown silk.

special mattress cover, more decorative than for everyday use. The bridegroom brings only a blanket, a knife and a few clothes to his new home. In Surin province, north-east Thailand, it is the bride's female relatives who weave the trousseau.

Marriage

In traditional village society a newly married couple will live in the compound of the bride's father. The compound may contain one or more houses depending on the number of close relatives living there. A matrilocal family system prevails, the youngest daughter and her husband inheriting the main family house and caring for her parents in old age. If a house is not already available, it will be built before the wedding and when completed is blessed by monks. The parents of the bride and groom appoint four village elders who perform lay ceremonies at the wedding service. One of their duties is to arrange the *kong toon* (financial settlement) and the small payment referred to as 'the payment for mother's milk' given to the bride's parents in acknowledgement of their role in rearing her. Included with the financial settlements are gifts of clothes and household textiles. In wealthy families the grandeur of the presents reflects the importance of the couple and their families.

Detail of a bridal bed sheet, Phichit province. Plain, hand-spun cotton warp and weft with supplementary-weft patterns. (*Right*) Red, yellow, lilac and blue silk, woven in diamond and zigzag patterns. (*Left*) Indigo cotton in diamonds, hooks, squares and zoomorphic patterns.

Carl Bock (1884, repr. 1986), an indefatigable European traveller who journeyed in Borneo, Sumatra, Burma, Laos and Thailand, described the wedding of a northern Thai prince which he witnessed in 1882:

About midday a band of musicians passed through the town, discoursing music . . . on tom toms, gongs and flutes accompanied by a party of singers chanting a monotonous song that resembled a funeral rather than a wedding march. Two dancing men followed . . . after them came servants and slaves carrying flowers arranged in different devices, some of them with great artistic taste and skill. The last floral device was a huge tower of flowers carried on a bamboo litter behind which came the Radjaput's umbrella bearer with a big red umbrella reared on a long silver shaft. More musicians preceded the prince's attendants who came walking two and two, some with gold and silver hilted swords drawn, others with arms reversed . . . and yet others bearing the inevitable gold or silver plate belonging to their master, such as tankards, betel boxes, spittoons, decanters etc. Finally the bridegroom himself, seated in a dog cart hauled not by his only pony . . . but by a dozen men who added to their labours by doing a considerable amount of shouting. The bridegroom himself . . . was dressed in a blue silk jacket embroidered with gold with a violet palai and a black velvet cap with a gold band. Behind the Radjaput came another revenue of servants two and two, each couple carrying between them a box of hard cash while a further instalment of the family plate succeeded. Next came a body of lancers, unmounted, followed by a fine display of nine large elephants, all tuskers, the leader carrying a huge red gilt howdah wherein were piled a quantity of gold embroidered cushions of different shapes, and of mattresses, constructed to fold up like a lady's fan, or rather like a Siamese book, zig zag fashion, all destined to form the furniture of the future establishment of the happy pair.

Such grandeur was reserved for royalty, their clothing and linen decorated with gold, the bed-linen often woven in silk, the marriage ceremonies elaborate. In the village, on the morning of the wedding, Buddhist monks will bless the bridal couple and their families. The monks proceed to the home of the bride who waits with the groom and attendants in front of an altar on top of which is placed a Buddha image, flowers, incense and candles. The monks sit to the side of the altar on mats and cushions which have been prepared for them and read from the scriptures. A white cotton cord is passed in a counter-clockwise direction from the Buddha image, out of a window and around the perimeter of the house. The cord encircles the house three times, and the end passes into a monk's bowl or an offering dish. The monks read from the scriptures and all those present inside the boundary set by the cord will receive blessings. The monks then sprinkle the bride and groom, their families and guests with lustral water which is a symbol of purification and gives extra blessings to the couple.

When the rites are completed the monks are offered food at a special table and presented with robes and other gifts. The monks then depart, and the bride changes into a wedding *phasin* and *pha sabai*, the groom into the clothes presented to him by the bride's parents. This set of clothes is called a *pha hawi haw* (Tambiah 1970). Wedding clothes and household textiles exchanged at times of marriage reflect the ethnic background of the family and their status. The richer the family the more silk, gold and silver thread will be used in the weaving.

In north-east Thailand a unique ceremony takes place after the monks have performed the preliminary religious rites. It contains both Buddhist and animist elements. Those taking part are the betrothed couple, appointed village elders and chosen wedding guests. A *phakhwan*, a cone-shaped offering dish of bananas, flowers, a boiled egg and a lump of rice, is offered to the spirits of the betrothed couple (Tambiah 1970). The *phakhwan* looks beautiful and contains food offerings to attract the spirits to the ceremony. Chanting begins to call the spirits and includes the following intercessions:

> Now I should like to call upon the *khwan* spirit of the beautiful bride to sit beside the bridegroom and the *khwan* of the bridegroom to sit beside the bride. Now the *khwan* have arrived . . . the bride has already made a bedroom for you. She is waiting for you. In the bedroom there are cloths of silk and cotton. Let the *khwan* of the bride return, and also the *khwan* of the groom that is wandering far away, please come back today (Tambiah 1970).

These intercessions continue while white cotton cord is attached to the offering dish and passed from the hands of the female officiants to the hands of the bride and groom, then to the male officiants and finally to the elders conducting the ritual. In some areas in north-east Thailand a *pha koma* (man's sash) is used instead of white cotton cord (verbal communication with villagers). The spirits, which have been summoned by the elders and are attracted to the beauty of the offering bowl, pass to the bride and groom via the blessed cotton cord or the sash. In the next part of the ceremony bamboo rings and pieces of unspun cotton are placed on the heads of the bride and groom, a candle is lit, and chanting continues. Guests bind the wrists of the couple with cotton cord to bring good luck, which completes the official rites, and family and guests enjoy a wedding feast.

Birth

When a woman is pregnant, a ceremony is held to give protection to her and the developing child. In this instance only elderly women conduct the rites. A cotton ring is placed on the pregnant woman's head, a candle is lit in front of her, and she is sprinkled with lustral water. A cotton cord is attached to a *phakhwan* offering bowl and passes through the hands of the elderly women to the pregnant woman. Chanting begins to summon the spirit who will protect the mother and child during delivery (Tambiah 1970).

Woven textiles are a protective symbol for a new-born child. If a baby girl is born, she is wrapped in a *phasin* worn by the mother during pregnancy. If the child is male, he is wrapped in a *pha sarong* belonging to the father. It is important that the *phasin* or *pha sarong* has been worn (verbal communication with villagers in north-east Thailand).

It was a custom, now no longer practised, that after delivery a mother spent up to seven days by a fire, which was believed to restore her strength. She lay on a special bed lined with bamboo and banana leaves which helped to retain a constant heat. Spirit cloths illustrated with magic symbols were hung around the bed at the eight major points of the compass; some were hung over the

Temple mural painting, Wat Phumin, Nan province. Gilded and lacquered offering bowls and dishes are used during Buddhist ceremonies, including weddings.

49

bed and others placed on the floor beneath it. Their purpose was to protect the mother against evil spirits while she endured the heat treatment. White cotton cord blessed by the monks marked the boundary of spiritual protection.

In north-east Thailand mothers sing lullabies which contain references to silk and cotton weaving (Peetathawatchai 1973).

FIRST LULLABY

Sleep baby sleep,
I will sing a lullaby.
Your father has gone to Central Thailand to trade cotton and silk,
When he returns he will buy fish for you,
It is hot, I will make a curry for you to help you grow strong,
Sleep baby, sleep like a log.

Temple mural painting, Wat Sra Bua Kaew, Khon Kaen province, depicting a man rocking a cradle made of an indigo sarong or *pha koma* suspended on a wooden frame. The inscription helps the viewer to understand this particular scene in the religious story. In north-east Thailand the inscriptions are in Pali, Sanskrit, Isan or central Thai lettering.

SECOND LULLABY

Sleep my child while I sing to you.
Sleep in the cradle while I rock you
I will spin yarn under the full moon and talk to the young men,
I will find a step father to care for you until you are grown
Your uncles and aunts have deserted us,
Although neighbours we are ignored,
They eat *pla buk* the size of a boat's stern but not a morsel will they share
They eat *pla sua* the size of an elephant's head but not a morsel will they give,
All we receive are *pla kaow* given as alms
The sky is lonely and vast with the stars and the moon
Oh, who will cut the grass to thatch the roof so you will live to later care for me.

A novice monk, with attendants, being carried in an ordination procession to the temple, Chiang Mai province. In north Thailand the novices are colourfully dressed; in the north-east they often wear white robes.

Novices and monks

As boys approach manhood they customarily enter a *wat* (monastery) for a period, taking their vows in the week before the beginning of Buddhist Lent and staying throughout the Lenten period of three months. The *wat* consists of a temple where villagers and monks worship together, a second temple where novices are ordained, accommodation where the monks live, and a cemetery at the western end of the complex. There may also be a school for village boys, a kitchen where villagers can prepare food for festivals, and outbuildings where ceremonial objects used in religious processions can be stored.

Villagers attend many religious ceremonies during the year, and the temple grounds are also used for travelling fairs, musical performances and plays. Elderly villagers spend many hours worshipping in the temple and sometimes sleep overnight during festivals.

51

A Buddhist monk conducting a house blessing ceremony in Bangkok.

In this way the temple provides a religious focus and is also a place where people can socialise.

A boy's female relatives may weave robes well in advance of his entering the monastery, an event anticipated with great pride. On the day of the ceremony novices process to the monastery, accompanied by their families and members of the village. In parts of north Thailand they are dressed in brightly coloured clothes with their faces painted, similar to Burmese tradition. They are borne shoulder high on a palanquin carried by the men of the village, preceded by offering bowls of flowers, joss sticks and candles. Some wear silk ceremonial blankets over the white robes. In north-east Thailand the aspiring novice marks the first stage of transition towards monkhood by discarding his everyday clothes for a special loin cloth, a *pha hang*. This is worn in the same pantaloon style as the *pha chong kaben*, passed around the waist, between the legs and tucked at the front or back. Woven in shot and plied silk using two- or three-colour yarns, the *pha hang* has a subtle, shimmering surface, not quite a pattern but not as simple as the plain weave of monks' robes. The *pha hang* is also used during funeral rites to cover the coffin of male members of the family. After funeral rites it is taken to the monastery for purification before it can be returned to the family.

A young man passes into the second stage of transition into the monkhood when he changes from the *pha hang* into white robes which he wears in the ordination procession. Whether dressed in simple white robes or the brightly coloured clothes of the northern tradition, the novice processes to the ordination hall. He enters, has his head shaved by one of the monks, and changes from white to saffron robes. The transition from layman to novice is complete when he takes the vows of poverty, chastity and obedience which govern the lives of all Buddhist monks. While most young men leave the monastery after three months, some stay to spend a lifetime ordained.

The monks and monasteries are supported by the local community: villagers pay for *wat* maintenance and help carry out any necessary repairs in co-operation with the abbot and monks. The monks are nearly all local men and thus association between *wat* and village is a close one. The women's role is to provide food each day and to weave robes and other textiles needed by the monastery. Monks are intermediaries for the laity to 'make merit'. This means that by making gifts such as textiles to the monks the people reach a happy and virtuous state of mind in this life and gain spiritual grace for the next.

The Buddhist festivals

The Buddhist festivals of Thailand are in harmony with the seasons of the rice cycle; Buddhist Lent coincides with the planting and early growth of the rice crop. According to the scriptures, the Lord Buddha decreed that monks should remain in their monasteries at prayer and not visit the villages where they might inadvertently tread on the new rice seedlings. The main Buddhist merit-making ceremony is held while the rice is maturing and ripening and field labour is light. Harvest celebrations and further merit-making ceremonies are held in February and March when the rice crop is safely stored in the family rice barn, built close to the house.

The four major Buddhist festivals when monks are presented with woven textiles are Khaw Phansa (the beginning of Lent), Org Phansa (the end of Lent), Bun Kathin (the merit-making ceremony held between the full moons of October and November) and Bun Phraawes (the grandest merit-making ceremony and village festival of the year). Many of the textiles mentioned in these ceremonies are described in detail in Chapter 6.

Khaw Phansa

On Khaw Phansa, the beginning of Lent, villagers give white cotton robes to the monks for wear during ritual Lenten bathing. These were made from undyed, hand-spun cotton woven in plain weave, although today machine-woven cloth is normally used.

Org Phansa

On Org Phansa, the end of Lent, monks are given cotton robes as a collective gift from villagers. A venerated monk may be presented with silk robes, the weaver selecting the finest silk filament from the cocoon. Silk robes have special significance for monks and laity, and some monks, through modesty, will decline to wear them. For example, the abbot of a temple in north-east Thailand was given a set of silk robes by the weavers of his village but he was too modest to wear them and passed them on to a venerated monk from a monastery nearby whom he judged worthy of silk (verbal communication with the abbot, Wat Po Ngam).

Bhun Kathin

Bun Kathin is the festival which marks the end of the monsoon rains in October, and the celebrations take place over two days. The monks have ended their retreat and novices are free to re-enter village society. On the first day gifts for the monks are prepared in a *hau kathin*, a wooden palanquin decorated with banana stems and paper streamers. There are gifts of money and food, a set of monk's robes, pillows and, occasionally, bed-linen. Woven banners and painted flags which will be carried in the procession are brought out of store and repaired if necessary. In the evening a small fair is held in the temple grounds. The following morning villagers line up in procession. This is an occasion for wearing their best clothes, the men in *pha chong kaben* or *pha sarong* and shoulder-sashes, while the women wear their best *phasin* and *pha sabai*. Today it is common to see men in trousers and patterned shirts with sashes worn at the waist and women in Western-style blouses with white machine-lace shoulder-sashes. In the procession to the temple men carry the palanquin and the banners and flags. Bringing up the rear is a band, with the women and children dancing as they go. On reaching the *wat* compound the procession circles the temple three times before entering. White cotton cord is passed round the outside of the temple, and all those enclosed will acquire merit during the ceremony (Tambiah 1970). The monk's robes which have been carried in the palanquin are presented to the abbot by a male village elder, and the other gifts are presented to the monks. The *kathin* ceremony ends with chanting from the scriptures.

Bun Phraawes

Bun Phraawes is the major merit-making ceremony of the year, and coming after the rice harvest is also a harvest festival. The temple interior and the grounds are decorated with colourful streamers and

A ceremonial banner from Wat Po Ngam, Khon Kaen province, being inspected before a temple ceremony by monks and villagers. The villagers in the foreground are wearing silk sashes, the man a plaid sarong. A monk in saffron robes stands in the background.

Detail of a ceremonial banner, Wat Po Ngam, Khon Kaen province. The banner has a plain cotton warp and weft. There are flat bamboo sticks inserted in the warp at intervals to create patterns and the name of the temple, which is in central Thai lettering.

Detail of a ceremonial banner, Nan province. White machine-spun cotton warp and weft with a supplementary-weft pattern of a temple woven in red, tan, green, purple and pink cotton.

pha tung banners. Inside the temple the decorations are of two types. Some are loosely structured, made of bamboo rods set at intervals between coloured yarns which are arranged in macramé-like patterns, the end-borders decorated with silver paper and tassels of coloured yarn. These decorations, which often resemble spiders' webs, are special to the Bun Phraawes festival and represent the association of the Buddha with the natural world in his last birth before reaching enlightenment. The second type of decorations are cotton or silk banners woven on a loom, which are hung around the altar where the Buddha image is displayed. They contain woven patterns of temples, ritual offering bowls, animals, birds and flowers. In order to hang straight they are stiffened with bamboo rods which are inserted at intervals in the weft. Outside in the temple grounds the banners are around 16 ft (5 m) in length and are flown on long bamboo poles so that they are clearly visible from a distance – one or two may be hoisted at the roadside to let passers-by know of the ceremony. In former times when the river was the main highway banners were also flown on the river bank. For the Bun Phraawes festival banners are also flown on bamboo poles set at fixed points to the north, south, east and west of the temple building. Baskets are placed on the ground at the foot of each pole, and during the religious rites, sticky rice, candles and flowers will be dropped into the baskets as offerings to the divine angels. In return it is believed the angels will bring good health and well-being to the village. Although all banners flown at Buddhist ceremonies contain religious symbols, the structure and patterns chosen vary according to the ethnic background of the weavers. These regional and ethnic variations are explored in Chapter 6.

The custom of the sacred colours

Besides celebrating the major festivals, the wearing of certain coloured textiles also marks the days of the week. This custom is thought to be linked with the court of Ayuthya where the people believed they were protected by seven guardian angels, each one associated with a day of the week and a specific colour. Red was for Sunday, cream for Monday, pink for Tuesday, green for Wednesday, orange for Thursday, blue for Friday, and purple for Saturday. This tradition continued when the capital of the kingdom moved to Bangkok, and during the reign of King Rama II (1809–24) the custom was reinterpreted in the writings of the court poet Suntornphu (Chumbala 1985).

For a wardrobe to be proper it must include the seven sacred colours:

SUNDAY – wear red, great luck will follow.

MONDAY – wear white, the secret of long life.

TUESDAY – mix blue and purple, you will be blessed with grace.

Detail of an animist textile, Chiang Mai province. The script and figures are drawn in ink on plain-weave cotton. There are squares and circles entwined with snakes, the outer circle with Lanna script, and combinations of letters and symbols believed to have spiritual powers.

WEDNESDAY – the day for green.

THURSDAY – wear orange with a stroke of yellow.

FRIDAY – be keen to battle in grey.

SATURDAY – all arrayed in purple.

Do not lack these rules proved holy.

The custom of the seven colours was observed by both sexes. In the National Museum, Bangkok, there is a collection of linen jackets in the seven sacred colours which were worn by King Rama IV (1851–68). The necessity for so many outfits was beyond the means of most people, and the custom became a symbol of wealth and authority. As fashions changed at court so the rules were modified. The custom in the reign of King Chulalongkorn (1868–1910) existed as follows:

MONDAY – pale yellow for the lower wrap (*pha chong kaben*) with pale blue or dark pink for the shoulder-sash (*pha sabai*).

TUESDAY – deep feather blue for the lower wrap and a shoulder-sash of red.

WEDNESDAY – iron grey or tin grey for the lower wrap and a shoulder-sash of yellow ochre.

THURSDAY – leaf green for the lower wrap with a blood-red shoulder-sash or orange lower wrap with a pale green shoulder-sash.

FRIDAY – deep blue lower wrap with a yellow shoulder-sash.

SATURDAY – purple lower wrap with a pale grey shoulder-sash.

White was the colour of mourning. The custom of the seven colours has slowly been abandoned, although there are still Thais who believe that wearing the colour of the day will bring good luck.

Textiles for protection

When a young man leaves his village to find work, to serve in the army, or for some other reason which keeps him absent for a prolonged period, his mother will weave a silk *pha sarong* as a parting gift. Believed to offer protection from harmful spirits, it acts as a reminder of family and home village. In north-east Thailand it was customary for a soldier to carry a *phasin* belonging to his mother into battle to protect him from serious injury (verbal communication with Acharn Suriya Smutkupt, Khon Kaen University). There are some animist textiles of plain, undyed cotton which have geometric symbols, mythical animals and ancient scripts drawn on the surface with black ink. These are believed to have protective powers: some, in former times, were taken into battle; others were used during animist rites.

Rites of exorcism

In Thai society Buddhism coexists with animism, a belief in the power of spirits who can influence human life. Individual spirits

A spirit-offering tray left in a lane bordering the village of Ban Fang, Khon Kaen province. The bamboo-plaited tray has silk cocoons tied to nine bamboo canes which are arranged around the rim. The contents are a ball of rice, a rice dessert, cigarettes, a betel nut, joss sticks, lustral water and candles.

have power over specific aspects of life and must be appeased according to custom. The spirit mediator of the village knows the rituals and procedures to be followed. Ancestral spirits, village guardian spirits, spirits of rice and of the rice fields, spirits of trees, swamps and woodlands are among those to be appeased. It is believed that spirits may be offended when villagers deviate from normal custom, for example, cutting down special village trees without first conciliating the guardian spirit of the village (Tambiah 1970). To placate offended spirits special offerings are made at an appropriate location. This may be within an individual house or compound, at a chosen site in the village or in a field, or in the surrounding countryside. In some instances offerings will include woven textiles or textile fibres.

One spirit offering seen at Ban Fang village, north-east Thailand, was left at the side of a lane. It consisted of a bamboo plaited tray approximately 15 inches (38 cm) square, decorated with nine sticks of bamboo on which silk cocoons were tied. Arranged on the tray were a ball of rice, a rice dessert, cigarettes, betel nut, joss sticks, lustral water and candles. Villagers said they did not know the significance of the silk cocoons, but these were included on the advice of the spirit mediator.

There is a more serious type of spirit which villagers believe takes possession of the body causing some form of mental illness. In this case the services of an exorcist are required. He will identify the malevolent spirit and carry out the ceremony of exorcism. This may include some worn clothing belonging to the afflicted which is used

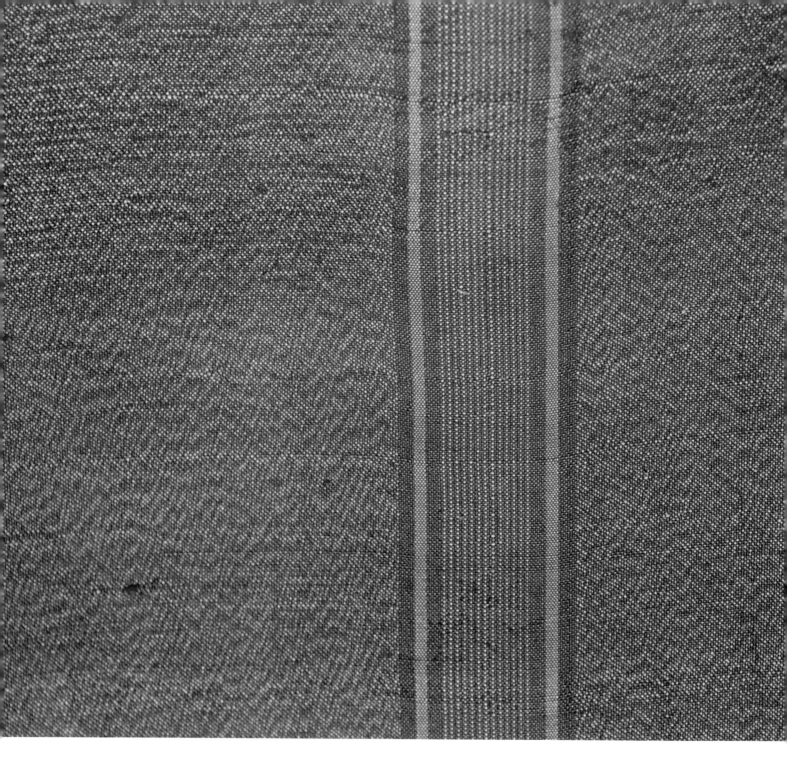

to lure the malevolent spirit away. The exorcist's fee may include textiles, such as a sash or a *pha sarong*.

Death

Textiles play a central role in funeral rites. When there is a death in the family the body is laid out at home in its best clothes and placed on a woven mat, the head resting on a pillow pointing to the west. Ritual items are placed at the head of the corpse, including a mattress, blanket and clothing, thought to be needed in heaven. White cotton cord is tied above the head and feet, and while the body is being laid out, some men will have gathered wood for the funeral pyre. When the preparations are complete the body is placed in a coffin, and the lid is covered with a *pha hang* for a male or a *phasin* for a female. The *pha hang* is described as a rites of passage cloth (lecture by Acharn Suriya Smutkupt, West Surrey College of Art and Design, Farnham, Surrey, 1990). The coffin is carried from the house to the cemetery in procession, led by chanting monks. At the cemetery there are further rituals and chanting, and when these are complete the textile cover is removed from the coffin. A male relative of the deceased may remove the *pha hang* with his teeth (verbal communication with Acharn Suriya Smutkupt). Monks and villagers then light the funeral pyre. Villagers return home, first visiting the temple for purification. The textiles used during the ceremony are also taken to the temple for purification. After several days, mortuary rites are conducted, and at their conclusion monks are presented with gifts of robes, pillows and blankets by the family of the deceased.

A strong relationship clearly exists between textiles, Buddhism and animism in ceremonial rites. It is also evident that for women woven textiles provide a means of gaining status in a religious and secular context. Today as fewer women learn to weave in Thailand and factory-produced textiles replace traditional hand-woven cloth, these complex relationships are fast disappearing.

Detail of a *pha hang*, Khon Kaen province. Red silk warp, plied green and tan silk for the weft, woven in plain weave with fine green and tan weft stripes on the end-borders.

3

SILK
AND COTTON
PRODUCTION

In Thailand the production of silk and cotton was the work of women who cultivated cotton and gathered silk moths from the wild to use as breeding stock for sericulture. They harvested materials from local plants and trees which they used to make dyes, and mordanted the yarn using river mud, plant extracts and local clays. They worked at their looms as other household duties allowed, stopping at the times of planting and harvesting the rice crop, when all able hands were needed in the fields. These traditions continue in some rural areas, but there have been many changes: in the cottage-industry sector men now help with the processing and dyeing of yarn, and many women have moved from their homes to employment in the handloom factories.

Cotton

When the Tai migrated into the valleys of Thailand they cleared the land to establish rice fields and grew cotton as one of the secondary crops. Cotton takes approximately seven months from planting to harvesting so that yarn for clothing and bedding can be produced in a relatively short time. Over the last two decades there has been pressure on land to yield high-value cash-crops such as tobacco and soya bean, and the cultivation of cotton in Thailand has declined.

Detail of a *phasin*, Nan province. Narrow bands of
cotton interspersed with rows of silver and gold
thread and bands of tapestry weave in
geometric patterns.

Above Three examples of *matmi* silk *phasin* produced in a village in Roi Et province.

Right Ba Sangda Bansiddhi of Chom Ton, north Thailand, seated among the skeined cotton which is processed, dyed and woven in her compound. She takes inspiration from traditional Thai weaving patterns and dye colours. A collection of Lanna textiles is displayed in front of her.

However, there is a demand for indigenous cotton from weavers who specialise in the production of hand-spun, hand-woven cloth. These areas include Chom Ton, Chiang Mai province, the Nan valley and Chiang Kham in north Thailand and Nong Khai in north-east Thailand.

Cotton is planted at the beginning of the monsoon season and harvested between December and February when the bolls are ready for picking. Indigenous cotton comes in two colours, cream and light brown. Bolls are left to wither on the plants, then the cotton is hand-picked and dried in the sun for about five days, after which it is ginned to remove the seeds and 'bowed' in a bell-shaped woven basket with a device shaped like a hunting-bow. The bow string is plucked rapidly to vibrate against the fibres and make them fluffy. When the fibres are sufficiently fluffed up, the cotton is rolled around a wooden dowel to produce elongated tufts the size of cigars, which are then rotated and the fibres twisted on a spindle to produce a continuous thread. The spinning-wheel used is like the Indian *charkha*: the operator sits on the floor turning the driving wheel by hand to rotate the spindle. The spun yarn is reeled on to a bamboo frame and wound into skeins to fit clay dye pots which hold 2–4 pints (1–2.5 l) of liquid. This describes cotton production as it occurs in a village setting; in the cottage-industry sector the

Ginning cotton, Nan province. The woman is wearing a typical Nan style *phasin*.

63

A woman reeling cotton in the area under a house at Chom Ton, north Thailand. Cotton yarn is rewound from large bamboo reels on to small bobbins which fit into wooden shuttles used for weaving.

cotton is machine-spun and skeined for large aniline dye vats. Many women today weave with machine-spun, ready-dyed cotton which they buy in the market.

Silk

In early village settlements silk moths were gathered from wild mulberry trees and bred seasonally. Today many women in north-east Thailand cultivate mulberry trees in their home gardens and keep regular breeding stocks of silkworms. The mulberry takes two to three years to establish, and the young trees are pruned and fertilised before the monsoon season when growth is rapid. The silkworm which is indigenous to Thailand is *Bombyx mori Linnaeus*: the cocoons are a golden yellow and produce thread with a rich slub and sheen which give Thai silk its unique appearance and texture. There are many native and native hybrid varieties; so far nineteen have been collected by the Thailand Department of Agriculture.* The names of native silk moths vary from place to place.

* The nineteen varieties so far identified are: Nang Noi, Nang Lai, Nang Luang, Na Noi, Nang Kiew, Nang Sew, PC. 1 (Pak Chong), RE.1 (Roi Et), CB. 9 (Chonnabot), Thai Surin, RE. 3, PC. 21, NK. 4 (Nong Khai), NK. 1, Phut Thai Song, CB. 2, Block Nang Sew, Nang Num, None Rue-See. (Data provided by Chainat Monaiyapong, North East Crop Development Project, 1988, Tha Phra, Thailand.)

The time for breeding silkworms is when the monsoon rains bring new leaf growth to the mulberry trees and women have free time after helping plant the main rice crop. Initial stock is obtained by barter from those who have bred silkworms out of season; this can provide an important source of income for poor families. In the first cycle the moths are allowed to hatch, and males and females are placed together on rattan trays and left covered with a cotton cloth. Around seven days after breeding each female lays 250–300 eggs which hatch about nine days later into tiny caterpillars, referred to as silkworms. The worms are laid on circular rattan trays lined with paper, and feeding begins three days after hatching. The worms are fed three times a day on finely chopped mulberry leaves which women gather fresh from their gardens or from plots on the outskirts of the village. When mulberry leaves are gathered from a distant plot they are wrapped in banana leaves to protect them from shrivelling in the hot sun. If a woman does not own enough mulberry trees to feed her silkworms, she may barter rice for an extra supply of leaves.

Silkworms need shelter from the sun and skilled labour to maintain the necessary standards of hygiene and care. The worms are fed chopped mulberry in the early morning, at noon and in the early evening. In some villages in the north-east the women take a lunch-time meal to the monks in the local monastery and then return home to feed the silkworms. Every day the paper lining the rattan trays is cleaned and changed and the worms graded and resorted by size on to new trays to allow room for growth. Silkworms are vulnerable to insect pests, especially parasitic wasps, flies and ants. To protect the worms from attack by ants and other crawling insects the rattan trays are stacked on wooden racks which are kept standing in water. To keep parasitic wasps and flies away the trays are covered with cotton cloths, often old sarongs. Extra vigilance is needed when the cloths are removed to clean and grade the worms. Recently new methods of protection have been introduced. These include simple nylon-mesh screens supported on bamboo frames which provide an insect-free enclosure about the size of a small garden shed. Inside there is enough room to clean, grade and feed the worms. Concrete rearing sheds with screened windows and doors are also available, although only to families who can afford the initial capital outlay and subsequent upkeep. Poorer families continue to raise silkworms in the traditional way.

It takes about thirty days to raise a batch of silkworms, and as they grow the number of feeds is sometimes increased to four times a day. This is done to make the worms grow faster, but many women with busy households just do not have the time for a fourth feed. When the worms are ready to spin cocoons they stop eating and develop a transparent look, which the women describe as 'ripe'.

A woman sorting and grading silkworms inside a screened shed which protects the worms from insect predators. Ban Hin Lad, Khon Kaen province.

Far right Reeling silk from the cocoons. Two grades can be seen on the reel – the outer, coarse filament and the inner filament. When all the filament has been reeled, the remaining silkworms may provide a raw snack for village children, or be cooked with spices and herbs to provide a protein rich dish. Ban Sawang, Khon Kaen province.

At this stage they are moved to large, circular, compartmentalised trays, called *jaw*, which are about 5 ft (1.5 m) in diameter. The ripe worms attach themselves to the wall of a compartment by secreting a small droplet of gum. First the preliminary web, called floss, is spun, and this forms the foundation for the main filament. The whole process takes two to three days. When spinning stops, the cocoons are removed from the *jaw* and stored in a basket covered with a cloth to prevent insect infestation. The cocoons must be reeled within ten days or the moths hatch and damage the silk filaments. Any cocoons which are damaged or infested are rejected before reeling begins, and some healthy cocoons are held back and allowed to hatch into moths to continue the breeding cycle.

When there is a good supply of cocoons ready for reeling, a small charcoal or wood fire is prepared. Some women prefer a log fire because they say it is easier to control the heat. A clay pot or metal cauldron of water containing silk cocoons is placed over the fire and the water temperature kept just below boiling-point. Hot water releases the silk filaments which are drawn up through a forked bamboo batten from between ten and twenty cocoons at a time and twisted to form a single silk strand. The strand then passes over a conducting reel and on to a bamboo spool or is reeled into a basket. An experienced silk reeler can tell if the denier alters by the feel of the thread as it passes through her fingers. If the denier feels thinner she will automatically attach additional filaments. Hand-reeled silk is rounded in texture and has a distinctive sheen which is important to the character of Thai silk. The roundness and regularity of the ply assure that the silk will dye to an even colour.

Reeling silk is a laborious process, taking approximately twelve hours to reel 0.5 lb (0.25 kg), and the women often sit in groups to

A woman sits reeling silk in the compound of her house at Ban Sawang, Khon Kaen province. In the background a baby is asleep in a cradle made from a length of material suspended on a wooden frame.

chat while they work. Silk is reeled into three grades. Filaments from the outer layer of the cocoon are relatively coarse and hairy and are skeined separately. Nowadays they are sold to outside buyers for weaving into soft furnishing fabrics. Filaments from the middle layer of the cocoon are the smoothest and easiest to reel. Those from the inner layer are very fine and can easily become tangled, requiring patience and concentration to prevent knots forming. Reeling inner silk filaments may be time-consuming but produces high-quality silk. Village weavers use both inner and middle silk on their looms.

The worms inside the cocoons provide a tasty snack for village children who stand and keep an eye open for the juiciest ones as they emerge from the cauldron. In poor villages silkworms provide an important source of protein for children and adults. To make a delicious dish the worms are ground to form a paste and mixed with chilli, garlic, salt and shallots, or they are roasted in banana leaves with herbs and spices. Any surplus worms are bartered in the village or sold in a local market.

Dyes and mordants

Until this century the plants and shrubs used for extracting dyes were harvested locally from forests and wastelands, or raised in home gardens. A few dyes were carried on the trade routes from China, but these did not reach remote villages. Today aniline dyes are available in markets throughout Thailand. In recent years there has been a revival of interest in vegetable dyes, and some master weavers and dyers have begun to specialise in producing a rich variety of colours using traditional recipes, mostly on cotton. Many of these fabrics can be bought through specialist retail shops, and it is often possible to visit the dyers in their workshops. However, in spite of this revival, aniline dyes are now used extensively, and it is only the elderly women who can remember using vegetable dyes and mordants. They can identify the trees and shrubs in the forest which were once the source of dyes and remember the preparation to extract the colours. In those days women had a vested interest in preserving trees and shrubs and they helped prevent unnecessary felling and over-grazing.

In the villages where vegetable dyes are still used an area under the house or in the compound is set aside for preparing dye baths, and the raw ingredients and utensils are kept there. Charcoal braziers are used to heat dye baths, and dye ingredients are mixed in earthenware pots. The recipes are difficult to record accurately because the dyers do not use weighing scales but estimate the size of the skeins in relation to the volume of unprocessed dyestuff. Questions about accurate weight by pound or kilo are met with amusement as dyers use volume of approximately one part cotton or silk to two parts dyestuff (for example, berries, roots, leaves,

Locally harvested farm and forest products, used for vegetable dyes and mordants, are left to dry or stored in baskets ready for processing. Chom Ton, north Thailand.

stems) as a guide. Preparation involves either soaking or boiling the raw dyestuff in water until the colour is extracted. The resulting liquid is filtered to remove sediment, and various acid or alkali ingredients are added, the correct amount determined by the colour, consistency, smell and taste of the solution.

Some women test their dye baths on small samples of yarn before adding whole skeins; experienced dyers say they just know when the dye is correctly balanced. Dyers are like cooks – they each have a favourite way of preparing the same basic recipe. In many cases the same dyes can be used for silk and cotton, but a greater depth of colour is achieved on silk when a mordant is not used. The ingredients added to the basic dyestuff are varied to create degrees of acidity or alkalinity. Dyers speak of their dye baths as either sweet or sour. For example, to create a dye bath for cotton a handful of tamarind leaves or an alkaline crystal bought in the market creates the correct flavour. An acid fruit may be added to dye baths used for silk, creating a sour taste.

Mordants are substances used to fix dyes. Today they are purchased in ready prepared packets from the market, but in former times they were obtained from local sources. To fix black, blue and yellow dyes on cotton the fibres were immersed in the mud obtained

69

Plant Dyes

COLOUR	BOTANICAL NAME	THAI/ENGLISH NAME	PART USED
red/pink	*Caesalpinia sappan*	*mai fang*/sappan wood	corewood
red/pink	*Areca catechu*	betel nut	nut
red	*Carthamus tinctorius*	*kham foi*/safflower	flowers
red	*Morinda citrifolia*	*yo pa*/Indian mulberry	wood, bark, roots
red	*Baccaurea sapida*	Burmese grape	wood
red	*Bixa orellana*	*khamsaed*/annatto	seeds
yellow	*Tamarindus indica*	*makham thai*/tamarind	leaves
yellow	*Garcinia mangostana*	*rong*/mangosteen	sap
yellow	*Cudriana javanensis*	*kae lae*/mulberry family	corewood
yellow	*Aegle marmelos*	*ma tum*/bael fruit tree	fruit, seedpods
yellow	*Curcuma longa*	*khamin chan*/turmeric	rhizome
yellow	*Nyctanthes abortristis*	night-flowering jasmine	corolla
yellow	*Rauwenhoffia siamensis*	*nom meo*	bark
yellow/brown	*Artocarpus integrifolius*	*khanun*/jackfruit	corewood
khaki	*Oroxylon indicum*	*pheka*/sword-fruit tree	bark
khaki	*Tectona grandis*	*mai suk*/teak	corewood
green	*Terminalia belerica*	*samoe phiphet*/myrobalan	bark, fruit
green	*Terminalia catappa*	*hu kwang*/wild almond	leaves, bark
green	*Ananas sativa*	*supparot*/pineapple	leaves
green	*Garcinia tinctoria*	*ma hud*	corewood
green	*Sesbania grandiflora*	*ke* or *ke ban*/leguminous tree	leaves
black	*Harrisonia perforata*	*si fan kon ta* or *kon ta*/bitter bark	fruit
black	*Piper methysticum*	*phrik*/pepper	root
black	*Canarium kerrii*	*kakoem*	fruit
black	*Diospyros mollis*	*ma kleua*/ebony	fruit
brown	*Rhisophora mucronata*	*kong kang bi yai*/mangrove	wood
brown	*Peltophorum inerme*	*nonsi*	bark
brown	*Acacia catechu*	*si siad*/cutch	wood
orange/gold	*Lawsonia inermis*	*thian king*/henna	leaves
orange	*Bixa orellana*	*khamsaed*/annatto	seedpods, leaves
blue	*Indigofera tinctoria*	*khram*/indigo	stem, leaves

Insect Dyes

red	*Lakshadia chinensis*	*krang*/shellac	insect resin

from buffalo wallows. In some areas silt from the local river bed contained the necessary fixing agents. In Nan province dyers used tree bark ash to fix red dye on cotton. In some areas silk fibres are mordanted in water containing rusted metal, although this appears to be a recent practice. A group of dyers from Khon Kaen province, north-east Thailand, were told about the properties of rusted water by a group of women from another province who they met ten years previously while on a pilgrimage to a Buddhist shrine. Many women said that religious gatherings were a good opportunity to meet weavers and dyers from other districts and exchange recipes and methods.

Cotton absorbs dye more easily if the yarn is soaked in cold water and pounded to make the fibres round and even. Silk undergoes treatment to remove the gum and clean the fibres; it is degummed in a preparation made from either banana-treetrunk ash or spinach-leaf ash dissolved in boiling water. The resulting solution is left to cool and then strained through a cotton bag. Silk skeins are boiled in the strained liquid, left to cool, then removed and hung to dry. After degumming silk, skeins are prepared for dyeing in liquid made from thorny vine root and water. About 20 in (50 cm) of dried thorny vine root are chopped to matchstick size and boiled in water. The resulting solution is left to stand for three days and then strained. The silk skeins are boiled in this solution, then removed and hung to dry without rinsing.

Many customs and superstitions surround the use of vegetable dyes. Dye vats were prepared in a special corner of the compound away from the house, dyes were not used on Buddhist holy days, and monks were not allowed near as they were believed to weaken the strength of the dyes. Pregnant or menstruating women were also believed to affect the dye baths (Peetathawatchai 1973). Restrictions surrounding the use of mordants include not talking while preparing the ingredients.

In the past a vast range of trees, plants and shrubs were used for dyes and mordants, but today only the elderly women can identify them. With the pressure on land for cash-crops, many woodland and scrub areas have been cleared and the habitat for dye plants has been lost. It is likely that the elderly women in the villages may be the last generation to know all the ingredients. However, with the increasing appreciation of hand-spun, vegetable-dyed fabrics, albeit in a small, specialist market, there is increased optimism that the old skills may not be completely lost.

Red

Red dye, *krang* (shellac), is secreted by the insect *Lakshadia chinensis* and produces red on silk and pink on cotton. The female insect deposits the resin along rain-tree branches (*Samanea saman*). To har-

Detail of a silk *phasin*, Phichit province. The *phasin* is tied and dyed in geometric patterns, the red dye produced from insect resin, *krang*. The Lao people who create this style of *phasin* are known as Lao Krang.

vest the resin women use long sticks to dislodge the deposits. The resin is left to dry in the sun and then ground to a coarse powder which forms the basic dye ingredient.

There are many recipes for dyeing cotton with *krang* – the following comes from a Tai Lue village in the Nan valley. A tamarind fruit, *makham* (*Tamarindus indica*), and the juice of a citrus fruit are brought to the boil with enough water to fill a dye pot (about 2–3 pints, 1–1.7 l). The liquid is reserved, skeined cotton is added and left for a few hours, then removed and hung to dry without rinsing. Meanwhile a dye bath is prepared from powdered *krang* which has been dissolved in boiling water, left to cool and strained. The prepared cotton yarn is immersed in the dye bath and turned frequently for two to three days to ensure an even colour; it is then rinsed and hung to dry. To fix the dye a mordanting agent is prepared from tree-bark ash. The woman who gave this recipe could not name the tree from which the ash was made, recognising it merely by its shape and colour. She said that while the bark is being burnt and when the ash is collected no one involved may speak or the ingredients will not fix the dye. Once the ash is collected it is dissolved in boiling water and the juice of a citrus fruit is added; it is then left

72

to cool and strained. The dyed cotton yarn is added and turned frequently to ensure all the fibres are treated evenly, then it is rinsed and hung to dry.

Krang was widely used as a dye in Thailand because it produces a rich red colour on silk. There is one Tai Lao group – referred to as the Lao Krang – who use the dye to great effect, producing strikingly beautiful red costumes. The dye is collected from the rain-trees as described in the previous recipe, ground to a powder and mixed with a little water to form a paste. The paste is put into a palm-leaf strainer and boiling water is slowly poured through it. The resulting red liquid is left to stand overnight. Meanwhile the juice of a citrus fruit, *makrut* (*Citrus hystrix*), is mixed with tamarind water, made by soaking a tamarind, *makham* (*Tamarindus indica*), in hot water and reserving the liquid. The mixture is added to the reserved red dye bath a little at a time and is tasted by the dyer until the correct flavour is reached. It must be neither too sweet nor too sour but what is described as a medium taste. When the dyer is satisfied with the flavour she heats the dye bath and adds the skeins of silk. They are turned until an even red colour is reached, then removed, rinsed and hung to dry.

An alternative recipe involves soaking the *krang* powder in water for three days and then straining the liquid through a loosely woven cotton bag to remove the sediment. Meanwhile a tamarind fruit is soaked in water overnight and the resulting liquid added to the strained dye solution with the juice of an acid fruit. As in the previous recipe the dyer tastes the dye bath for the correct flavour. When the taste is right the silk yarn is added and boiled in the dye bath until the skeins are evenly dyed. To increase the depth of colour the quantity of *krang* powder is increased in relation to the other ingredients, and the dye bath can be boiled down to make it more concentrated.

Some dyers use a wood, called *sellac* in northern dialect, which produces a subtle red-brown colour on cotton but is prone to fading. The bark is cut into slithers about 4 in (10 cm) in length and boiled in water for at least one hour. The resulting liquid is strained and reserved. Cotton yarn is added and boiled until the dye is absorbed into the fibres. To fix the dye a mordant is prepared from the juice of a citrus fruit, salt, pork fat and water. The yarn is boiled in this solution, then rinsed and hung to dry.

Indigo

Indigo, *khram* (*Indigofera tinctura*), is a plant used to dye cotton for clothing and bedding. In Thailand it is not used for dyeing silk. Indigo was planted with cotton as a secondary crop following rice, but the pressure on land for cultivating cash crops has meant that it is grown only in areas where there is a specialist demand for

Detail of a cotton *phasin*, Khon Kaen province. The *phasin* was tied and dyed in an indigo dye bath to create *matmi* patterns. Isan Culture Museum, Khon Kaen University.

hand-woven, indigo-dyed cloth – for example, Nong Khai, north-east Thailand, and Chom Ton, north Thailand.

The following method for preparing indigo dye was collected from a village where the women were cultivating indigo in plots of about one quarter of an acre (0.6 ha). When mature, the plants are cut and tied in bundles and soaked in large ceramic jars of water. The indigo is cut before evening when the dew falls or the dye will not be easily extracted from the leaves (verbal communication with Ba Sangda Bansiddhi, a master weaver and dyer from Chom Ton province, north Thailand). The bundles of indigo plants are left in the jars of water to ferment for three days and are stirred occasionally. The decomposing leaves are squeezed to extract the dye and then discarded. Fresh indigo plants are added to the jars and left to ferment for a further three days. The leaves and stems that have not rotted down are again squeezed and discarded.

Lye is beaten into the strong-smelling residual liquid which then turns blue. Dyers gauge the amount of lye by the colour and smell: the ratio is approximately one part lye to five parts indigo. Once the lye has been added the indigo liquid is left to stand for two days, allowing the sediment to settle. The top liquid is then poured off, and the indigo sediment is stored as a paste until a dye bath is to be prepared. Many women buy indigo in paste form from their local markets. Today lye is also available commercially, but in former times it was made from snail shells and kapok-tree bark, burnt to ashes. Some villagers specialised in this production and bartered with the indigo dyers for rice or another local commodity.

To prepare a dye bath the indigo paste is stirred into a solution made from tamarind-tree ash dissolved in water. This starts the fermentation process and the dye becomes active. Once fermentation starts it is sustained by adding ingredients such as sugar-cane, tamarind or acid fruit to the dye vat. Skilled dyers have their own recipes to maintain the correct pH level which they test by tasting. When the dye bath is ready, damp cotton yarn is added for about fifteen minutes and stirred frequently. The yarn is then removed without rinsing and dried in the shade. To obtain a darker colour the yarn is redipped – up to ten times if a rich blue-black is required – and the yarn is rinsed after the final dye bath. Between each dip the dye bath must be fed and fermentation allowed to restart, a time lapse of about twelve hours. The constant dipping and redipping of the yarn leave indigo dyers with hands and arms stained blue.

Black

The old method for making black dye was from ebony berries. Thai women cultivated ebony (*Diospyros mollis*) in their gardens or harvested the berries from trees around the village. First the ripe berries

Detail of a cotton *phasin*, Nan province. The *phasin* has plain bands of pink and brown cotton alternating with bands of indigo *matmi*. The pink dye is made either from *krang* or *mai fang*, sappan wood. The brown dye was made from tree bark.

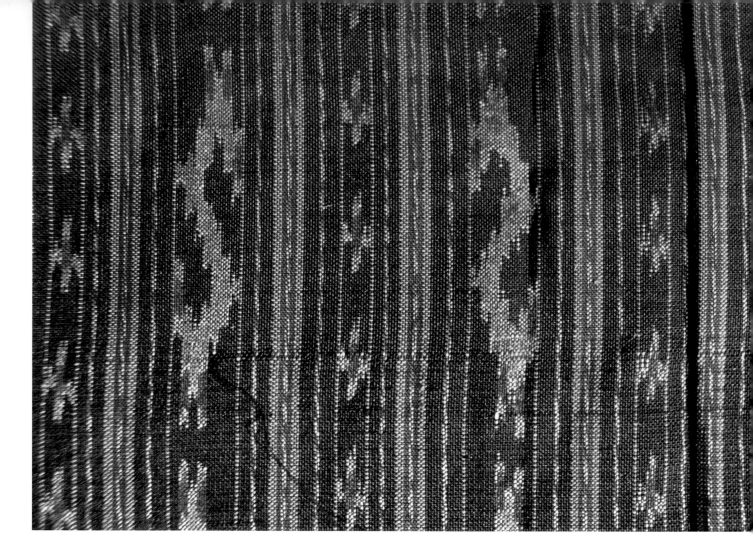

Detail of a silk *phasin*, Roi Et province. The serpent pattern alternates with fine weft stripes. Isan Culture Museum, Khon Kaen University.

were crushed to a pulp and mixed with lye, then water was added in measured amounts and stirred until a smooth liquid was produced. Damp skeins of cotton were immersed in the liquid for three days and turned frequently to ensure the yarn was dyed evenly. After three days, when the fibres were black, the cotton was taken out of the dye bath and squeezed to remove excess moisture. In the villages of north-east Thailand where ebony dyeing was common the women made lye from a species of large snail which they collected from local streams. The snail shells were burnt to ash and mixed with wood ash from the kitchen fire. To mordant the cotton it was laid out in damp skeins on the garden soil and turned to ensure all the yarn was evenly coated. The skeins were then taken to the river bank and kneaded in clay sediment, and finally rinsed in clear river water and hung to dry. The above method was used for cotton yarn, but ebony berries can also be used to dye silk. A recipe for a mordant was not obtained, which may mean the dyers do not use one. Today commercial dyes have largely replaced the use of ebony berries, or women rely on many dips in an indigo dye bath to produce a blue-black colour.

Yellow
Yellow dye is made from turmeric, *khamin* (*Curcuma longa*). The roots of the turmeric plant are ground to a powder and mixed with water

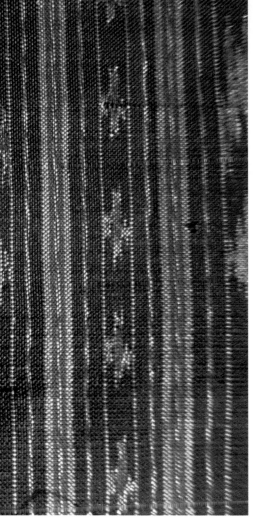

to form a paste. More water, a few pinches of salt, and some seed-pods, *ma tum* (*Aegle marmelos*), are stirred in and the resulting liquid left to stand overnight. Cotton yarn is added and stirred frequently to ensure the fibres dye evenly. The skeins are then rinsed and hung to dry. Today the cotton is mordanted with an alum solution obtained in the market, but the traditional method was to soak the fibres in the smooth mud collected from buffalo wallows. To dye silk yarn with turmeric the juice of an acid fruit is added to the dye bath.

Before the advent of aniline dyes, monks' cotton robes were dyed according to the rules laid down in religious texts. Bright colours were forbidden, and a dull yellow-brown was considered correct. This colour was achieved with dye from the jackfruit tree, *khanun* (*Artocarpus integrifolius*). Before the robes were dyed they were mordanted in a preparation made from cow dung, fine mud from the river bed and plant extracts. The dye was prepared by slicing core-wood of the breadfruit tree into fragments and boiling them in water to extract the dye. The mordanted robes were immersed in the dye bath until they reached the required shade of dull yellow-brown (Suvatabandhu 1964).

Secondary dyes
Yarn can be dyed in a sequence of dye baths to create secondary colours, for example:

  A red dye bath made with shellac followed by a blue dye bath made with indigo produces purple.

  A yellow dye bath made with turmeric followed by a blue dye bath made with indigo produces green.

  A yellow dye bath made with turmeric followed by a red dye bath made with shellac produces orange.

  A grey dye bath made with ebony berries followed by a yellow dye bath made with turmeric produces khaki.

Matmi
Dyeing one colour over another is a technique used in Thailand for making *matmi* (ikat) patterns. The technique involves tying and dyeing sections of weft yarn to a predetermined colour scheme or pattern before weaving. The areas of yarn which are tied resist the dye baths. Traditionally banana-tree twine was used for the ties, but today it has been replaced by nylon string. To create weft *matmi* the size of a woman's *phasin* a wooden device called a *lakmee* is used. This consists of two wooden dowels set apart at opposite ends of a rectangular board to the same width as a *phasin*. The yarn is tensioned backwards and forwards across the width of the *lakmee*, and a woman then sits and ties the weft in the pattern required. To produce a pattern of more than two colours the yarn is tied and

Silk yarn tied into *matmi* patterns is seen hanging to dry. Before the advent of nylon banana stems were used to make twine for ties. Chonnabot, Khon Kaen province.

dyed, then retied and redyed or has extra ties added for each colour. Impregnation of the principal colours takes place in a dye bath, but for small areas of colour the dye may be added with a brush when the weft threads are tensioned back on to the *lakmee*. When the dyeing processes are completed the patterned weft is wound on to a bamboo frame ready for reeling. After reeling, the bobbins are used in strict sequence in order to weave the pattern correctly. To keep them in order the bobbins are often strung on to a length of twine. The dyeing of complex weft *matmi* patterns for ceremonial dress is undertaken by skilled weavers and involves intricate tie patterns and numerous dye baths.

Warp threads may also be tie-dyed before weaving. Warp *matmi* is believed to have preceded weft *matmi* as a method of creating patterns in Thailand. This is evident from the warp *matmi* cotton costumes worn by the Lawa who settled in Thailand centuries before the Tai arrived. Weft *matmi* is believed to be part of a later court tradition.

Cloth finishes

A number of plant substances are used in the finishing process. To protect against fading and to give silk a lustrous sheen it is soaked in

A woman tying *matmi* patterns into silk yarn, tensioned on a *lakmee* frame. Khon Kaen province.

Matmi-patterned silk yarn on a large bamboo reel. The yarn will be wound on to small bobbins, woven in sequence to create the patterns. Chonnabot, Khon Kaen province.

a preparation made from the leaves and stem of a plant resembling spinach and identified by villagers in Ban Hin Lad, Khon Kaen province, as *phak hom*. The plant is burnt to ashes which are then dissolved in boiling water. The resulting liquid is strained through a loosely woven bag. Silk is immersed in the solution for a few minutes, then shaken and hung to dry. An alternative recipe uses the ash obtained from burnt sesame bushes, *Sesamum indicum*, after the seeds have been removed. The ash is dissolved in boiling water as in the previous recipe. Many women say they prefer to use the *phak hom* recipe, as the sesame preparation makes the silk too shiny.

Commercial dyes

Vegetable dyes and natural substances for mordants were used exclusively in Thailand until the nineteenth century when synthetic chemicals were introduced. There are no precise dates for aniline dyes reaching Thailand, but it is thought that a purple aniline dye was first imported into China in about 1870 followed soon after by cerise pink. These two dyes were carried on the trade routes to Thailand where they appear to have been used first for the *teen jok* borders on women's *phasin*. By the middle of the twentieth century aniline dyes were common, except in the more remote rural areas.

79

4

◆

LOOMS
AND WEAVING
TECHNIQUES

Detail of a Phu Tai *pha prae wa*, Kalasin province. The warp and weft are woven in red silk. The supplementary weft is composed of orange diamonds and linear patterns, filled with floral designs in blue, green and white silk. The sash was woven with the wrong side facing the weaver, the patterns either picked by hand or using shed sticks.

When the weaving season gets under way the villages resound with the clack of working looms which are set up in the space under the house. There is often no special flooring – looms rest on the bare earth which extends throughout the compound. They share the space under the house with agricultural implements, fishing nets and baskets, and often with racks of drying farm produce such as sweet corn and tobacco. Women work at their looms intermittently between household chores and farm labour. There is more time for weaving after the rice is planted and again after the harvest. Even in these times of relatively light labour there are still chickens and pigs to be fed, the household to run and possibly the rearing of silkworms. As the loom is set up in an open area under the house it is possible to keep an eye on the children and animals and deal with traders and visitors while weaving. Other activities may also be accommodated – perhaps a hairdressing salon run by one of the family or a small shop. In one village several looms were set up beside a slatted bamboo enclosure which served as the village hairdressing salon. Ladies strolled in for a set, chatting to the weavers while their hair was drying.

In Thailand there is active support and imaginative promotion of the handloom sector. In some villages, especially in poor rural areas, retailers provide looms and yarn to women who cannot afford the initial outlay to buy their own. These women are paid piece rates. Some charitable organisations also supply looms to weavers, and take the finished products and market them through charity shops in Thailand or overseas by catalogue and mail order. There is an important cottage-industry sector where women work in small handloom factories, the goods available from a shop on site or

A loom set up under a village house at Ban Don Chai, Nan province. At the bottom of the stairway are the occupant's shoes which have been removed before going up to the house.

through retail outlets in the country and abroad. In some areas there are master weavers who produce individual, high-quality silk pieces often commissioned by wealthy customers in Bangkok or abroad.

The loom and its accessories

In the settled farming communities of Thailand the traditional way of tensioning a warp is on a standing loom. The closest loom in size and structure to the Thai loom is the Burmese frame loom, and the warp is tied on the wooden beam above the weaver's head (Innes 1957). Although they vary in size, the average Thai loom is about 12 ft (3.6 m) long, 4½ ft (1.4 m) wide and 4½ ft (1.4 m) high. Looms are simple in construction with tongue-and-groove joints so that if there is competition for space under the house they are easily dismantled and stored when the weaving season is over. In some areas weavers use a loom with the warp wound round a board at the far end, referred to by Ling Roth (1918, repr. 1977) as a Malay loom. In the commercial sector a modified Burmese loom has been developed. The warp is held at the back of the loom on a circular warp beam with a ratchet device so that it can be rolled evenly forward as the weaver requires. There is a similar device at the front of the loom on to which the newly woven cloth is rolled.

The purpose of a loom frame is to provide tension for the warp. To create space in the warp so that the weft may be interlaced involves the use of a shedding device which is provided by heddles. Each heddle is looped around an individual warp thread. The heddles are connected to each other by cord held within a frame of

Right A woman working at a loom, set up under the house. The loom frame was constructed by a local carpenter and can be easily dismantled if the space under the house is needed for some other purpose. The heddle shafts and foot pedals are made of bamboo; the beater frame is carved wood. Khon Kaen province.

Below and page 85 Wooden shaft pulleys. The two carved with an elephant and a pig are from north Thailand and were originally painted. The two with *kinnari* figures are from north-east Thailand and are polished wood. Photo Addison Castle.

bamboo rods called a heddle shaft. The heddle shaft is attached to the top of the loom frame by cord which passes through pulleys. Under the warp the heddle shaft is attached to a bamboo treadle. The simplest arrangement is for the loom to have two heddle shafts to create plain weave. The weaver depresses the bamboo treadles in turn to lift alternate heddle shafts and create shed and counter-shed. In the Thai loom the back beam is set higher than the front beam which helps create a good shed. For complex weaves the number of heddle shafts may be up to sixteen. Heddles were traditionally made of cotton, although nylon is now widely used.

The weaver passes the weft through the shed with the aid of a shuttle. Wooden shuttles are made in varying lengths – up to 10 in (25 cm) for fine tapestry weave and 20 in (51 cm) for plain weave. They are carved in a long curved shape with a smooth surface which passes swiftly through the warp when thrown. Some have decorative carving around the bobbin holder. After each line of weft (called a pick) is inserted, the weaver beats in with a beater which is attached to the loom frame and contains a reed made from palm wood. The carving of palm-wood reeds requires the precision of a craftsman. There are a variety of gauges: fine silk thread requires *fuum kan*, teeth close together; while thick cotton requires *fuum saa*, teeth wide apart (Lefferts 1978). With frequent use palm-wood reeds develop a smooth patina which the weavers say produces a good beat. In the last few years metal reeds have been introduced which are twice the price of palm-wood reeds but do not need replacing so often. However, the metal is prone to rust in a humid climate and therefore needs more care. Weavers have their own preferences, some using metal reeds for a dense cloth, others preferring the beat of the lighter palm-wood reed.

All traditional weaving equipment is simple and practical, but many pieces reveal the creative talents of the carpenters. Shaft pulleys are carved in a variety of forms including elephants, rabbits, horses and *kinnari* (a mythical being of Thai legend, half-human, half-bird). Some are painted with geometric patterns, others are varnished or polished. There appear to be individual styles of carving in different areas of Thailand. The beaters which contain the reeds are decorated with floral and plant motifs with carved end-scrolls. Spool winders and spinning-wheels are also carved with floral and plant

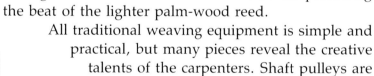

motifs; in north-east Thailand the *naga* (mythical snake) is a popular image on the end of spool winders.

Preparing the warp and weft

Before weaving begins the yarn for warp and weft is prepared to the required lengths. To prepare a warp for the loom skeins of yarn are transferred from bamboo reels on to a warping frame with a group cross to help keep the threads separated. The number of times the warp passes around the warping frame dictates the width. The length of the warp will depend on the number and length of the textiles to be woven, somewhere between 14 ft (4.3 m) and 30 ft (9 m) being the average. If a very long warp is required, it may be prepared in the village lanes. The next stage is to thread the warp through heddles and beater. For plain weave the weaver will select a two-heddle harness, for twill weaves she usually requires from three to eight heddle shafts. Weavers store heddle shafts and reeds together in sets of the same width with the end-threads of the previous warp left in place. Most weavers keep a selection to weave a variety of textiles for clothing and household use. If a woman does not own a particular set, she can usually borrow from someone in the village. When not in use the heddle shafts and beater are often suspended together under the house or from the rafters in the roof. Once the weaver has selected a set of the right size, and with the correct number of shafts, she ties each new weft thread in sequence to the end-threads left from the previous warp. This is an ingenious short cut to save completely rethreading heddles and reed every time a new warp is set up. When all new and old warp threads are joined, the ties are daubed with rice water to reinforce the knots and the new warp is drawn evenly through both heddles and reed. While she is making the ties the new warp has to be kept free of tangles; it is often wound carefully in a cloth or suspended from a house beam with just the end-threads hanging down.

Once the warp is threaded through the heddles and reed, it is suspended from the loom frame by cords attached to pulleys. The end warp farthest from the weaver passes across the top of the loom frame, over the supporting beam opposite the weaver, and passes back to be tied above the weaver's head. The near end of the warp is attached to the cloth or breast beam. When a Malay loom is used the warp is rolled around the warp beam which is suspended from the supporting beam at the back of the loom.

To prepare a weft, yarn is rewound from skeins on to bamboo reels by means of a wooden reeling device. It is then rewound on to bobbins of a size to fit the shuttles required for a particular weave. The operator preparing the spools sits on the floor keeping the reeling device steady with her foot. For weaving *matmi* the spools of dyed weft must be kept in strict order or the pattern will be

85

A woman tying old and new warp threads together. When they are all tied in the correct sequence, they are daubed with rice water to reinforce the knots, and the new warp is drawn evenly through both heddles and reed. Ban Chai Sor, Khon Kaen province.

distorted. This is achieved by threading the bobbins in sequence on to cotton thread with a bamboo rod at each end to secure them.

The weaving patterns

Plain weave

The simplest method of weaving is passing weft thread over and under each warp thread, then under and over on the following line. The structure which results is called plain weave. In order to create variants the warp and weft yarn can be of different colours and plies, and the yarn can be woven in a dense weave or in a more open weave with fewer threads per inch (2.5 cm). Sometimes yarns of different colours are plied together and woven as one. If the warp and weft are of the same ply and equally spaced, then the resulting cloth is said to be balanced plain weave. This is a popular weave for producing unpatterned indigo cotton which is cut for making clothes, especially farmers' shirts and trousers. It is also used in the weaving of many cottons and silks sold by the yard or metre. If the warp is a different colour from the weft, the resulting cloth is described as shot, a popular method of weaving silk to produce a shimmering effect. In north-east Thailand weft *matmi* is usually woven in plain weave, although twill weave is also used.

If the number of warp threads per inch (2.5 cm) is more than the number of weft threads, then the cloth is called warp faced. This arrangement is often used for warp *matmi* so that the pattern is dominant over the plain weft yarn. It may also be used when there are plied yarns or stripes in the warp. If the number of weft threads is more than the warp threads, then the cloth is called weft faced. This may be used for weft *matmi* and supplementary-weft patterns.

Float weave

When the warp and weft do not interlace in a simple over one/under one plain weave, then either warp or weft threads skip or float over one or two threads before being interwoven. When the float is patterned into a diagonal, it is known as twill weave. Twill weave is identified by the ratio of threads passing over and under the warp. The common ratios are 1:2, 1:3 and 1:4. In north-east Thailand float-weave patterns sometimes involve the use of two shafts for a plain weave binding, and in addition the warp is threaded through an extra set of shafts which are lifted in sequence to create a float-weave pattern resembling a simple geometric damask. There may be up to sixteen shafts depending on the pattern. This technique may have originated from ancient Chinese weaving traditions.

Supplementary weft

The weaving of patterns with a supplementary weft is known in Thailand as *khit* or *muk*. Supplementary-weft patterns are woven

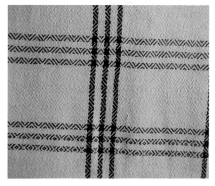

Detail of a cotton blanket from Khon Kaen province. The blanket is woven in a diamond float-weave pattern, in plain cotton with black stripes set at intervals to form a simple check. Isan Culture Museum, Khon Kaen University.

A woman hand-picking patterns using a wooden sword, which she is inserting into the warp. Ban Chai Sor, Khon Kaen province.

A vertical string-heddle harness suspended on the loom frame at right angles to the warp. The pattern has been picked into the vertical strings using bamboo shed sticks. The strings of the harness are connected to individual warp threads by string loops. The system is set up close enough to the weaver so that she can operate it on her own from the front of the loom. The resulting supplementary-weft pattern can be seen on the cloth beam. Ban Don Chai, Nan province.

into plain weave or in a variety of twill patterns requiring up to eight heddles. One of the oldest methods involves hand-picking patterns row by row using a wooden sword to create a shed for the insertion of a supplementary weft between rows of plain weave. Today some weavers still hand-pick patterns in this way, but most prefer a predetermined shed-selection process in which shed sticks or supplementary string heddles inserted in the warp accelerate and simplify the task of weaving. Shed sticks are commonly used to produce single images – for example, a temple, an elephant or a horse. In this case the sticks are inserted sequentially into the warp. If a mirror image is to be woven, the shed sticks are inserted sequentially until the middle of the pattern and then the sticks are inserted in reverse order. Floral and geometric patterns can also be woven in this way.

The technique of using a sequence of shed sticks to preselect the pattern of a supplementary weft is incorporated in a much more complex loom which can be found in some villages of north and north-east Thailand. Here the sticks are interwoven in a string harness which is set at a right angle to the warp, tensioned between

Above A weaver using shed sticks to
create patterns of supplementary
weft. The rows of sticks can be seen
in the warp. The weaver uses a
bow-shaped frame to keep the
warp threads level and evenly
spaced. Chom Ton, north Thailand.

Right Side view of a loom showing
a vertical string-heddle harness
dissecting the warp. Ban Lao
Kiawnlung, north-east Thailand.

the upper and lower extremities of the loom frame. The intersection of the ground weave is controlled by two shafts which the weaver activates by treadles. The pattern selection and creation of the shed for the supplementary weft is operated by one or two assistants attendant at the far end of the loom. However, if the loom frame is small and the harness close enough to the weaver, she may undertake the whole procedure on her own. There are string-harness systems operated by one woman only in numerous villages in the Nan valley, whereas harnesses with three operators are common in north-east Thailand.

To set up the loom the pattern to be woven is first picked row by

Cotton *jok* weaving, with the wrong side of the pattern facing upwards. The weavers working in this village in Chiang Mai province were supported by one of H. M. Queen Sirikit's handicraft projects. The textiles are marketed through the charitable foundation's Chitralada shops.

row into the vertical string harness using bamboo shed sticks. The strings of the harness are connected to individual warp threads by string loops. To operate the system a weaver's assistant moves the first shed stick down towards the warp. A wooden sword is inserted into the shed created by the lowered stick; the sword is then flipped on its side and drawn forward towards the cross to widen the counter-shed and allow insertion of a supplementary-weft yarn. While the shed stick remains in the harness above the warp, another stick is inserted into the harness below the warp in the same shed.

Detail of a silk *teen jok*, San Pathong, north Thailand. The refined geometric patterns, in multicoloured silk and gold thread, were hand-picked with the wrong side of the work facing the weaver.

The upper shed stick can then be removed. The weaver then inserts into the cloth one pick of plain ground weave. To continue the pattern the next shed stick in the harness is lowered towards the warp and the whole process is repeated. When only one stick is left in the upper part of the harness, the process is reversed – that is, sticks are moved from below to above the warp following the same principle of shed selection. Thus a mirror image pattern is created. The process continues with the shed sticks passing in sequence above and below the warp until the number of pattern sets required

91

A selection of silk *matmi* patterns, woven in a village near Khon Kaen. Each pattern has a name: *clockwise from top left* hook, turtle, small diamond, python, squid, water melon and diamond.

are completed. Some women keep the string harness intact when the work is finished, others dismantle it.

The most refined supplementary-weft technique is called *jok*, a Thai word meaning 'to pick'. Patterns are formed by the use of fine multicoloured silk, gold and silver threads. They are introduced into the ground weave as discontinuous supplementary-weft yarns and often worked with the reverse side of the fabric facing the weaver. The patterns are picked using the fingers or with the aid of a porcupine quill; a bow-shaped tool helps to keep the warp threads level and evenly spaced. The *jok* technique is used most frequently in the weaving of narrow widths of approximately 7 in (17.8 cm) to decor-

Above right Weaving a combination pattern of supplementary weft and tapestry weave. The small shuttles of white, pink and blue cotton are woven in isolated motifs to create tapestry-weave patterns which border a white, floral supplementary-weft design.

ate the hems of women's *phasin*. This distinctive hem is called *teen jok*. The patterns are so fine and intricate that a skilled weaver will take three to six weeks to complete one piece.

Tapestry weave

Tapestry weave, called *ko*, is a plain weave of discontinuous weft. The weaver keeps a quantity of small shuttles of yarn in front of her and weaves isolated motifs of contrasting colours which together form the cloth structure. In some regions the technique is used together with supplementary-weft patterns for women's *phasin*. These patterns are clearly discernible in the temple mural paintings of Wat Phumin and Wat Nong Bua, Nan, an area where tapestry weave is common.

Matmi

Patterns can be created by tie-dying yarn before weaving, a technique known generally as ikat but called *matmi* in Thailand. The method of dyeing the yarn is explained in Chapter 3. Today the majority of weavers make the pattern ties in the weft, but there is a tradition of warp *matmi* among a minority group, the Lawa, who wove warp *matmi* for their *phasin*. Normally weft *matmi* is woven with two shafts in a plain-weave construction. However, occasionally three shafts are used creating a 1:2 twill, the pattern on the weft-faced side giving a beautifully clear and bright impression.

93

5

THAI COSTUMES

The people of Thailand wear brightly patterned costumes. Against a background of green rice fields the geometric patterns and shimmering colours create a stunning picture. On holy days groups of women on their way to the temple walk in line along the earthen ridges that divide the fields, their woven ankle-length skirts providing brilliant flashes of colour in the sunlight. Men walk with equally colourful shoulder-sashes. In the hot season when the land becomes dry and dusty the costumes provide welcome relief from the otherwise monotonous grey-brown landscape. For work in the fields the clothes are plainer, often made of indigo-dyed cotton or simple plaid and striped cotton. The elderly wear muted colours and *matmi* woven in rich, dark patterns. At court brilliant silks decorated with gold and silver thread were worn by royalty and senior officials, the most lavish costumes reserved for those of the highest rank, as decreed by the king.

Textiles are not easy to conserve in the heat and humidity of the Thai climate. The earliest evidence of costume styles and textile patterns is taken from terracotta and stone figurines. These portray men and women wearing rectangular lengths of fabric draped around the body and tucked at the waist with a pleat or knot. The

Temple mural painting, Wat Phra Singh, Chiang Mai province, depicting a country scene of women traders in Lanna costume. They wear sashes thrown loosely over their shoulders and *phasin* with horizontal stripes in the main panels and plain red hem borders. The attendant men are wearing scant loincloths to show off their tattooed legs, with sashes in the same style as the women. They are smoking local cheroots.

fabric is used in a variety of ways, like a simple sarong, as a short loincloth, an ankle-length skirt, or draped to form loose pantaloon-style trousers. The fabric appears to be dense and hang stiffly or is thin and filmy, revealing the shape of the body underneath. With this lower garment there is a shoulder-sash which is tied and draped to cover the chest or partially expose it. Elaborate jewellery was often worn with this simple costume. Figurines of the Dvaravarti period (sixth to eleventh centuries AD) portray female figures wearing tight-fitting ankle-length skirts with decorative necklaces and bracelets and a sash over one shoulder in the style of a *pha sabai* (Wat Ku Bua, Ratburi province). From the Śrivijayan period (eighth to thirteenth centuries) stone figurines are depicted in similar ankle-length skirts with head, neck, arms and torso covered in elaborate head-dresses, bracelets, necklaces and other jewellery (National Museum, Bangkok).

Bronze figures from the Śrivijayan period portray women dressed in loose, mid-calf-length trousers made of semi-transparent material and metal waist-belts. They wear elaborate head-dresses and large earrings which hang to the shoulder. Men wear loincloths or draped sarongs and simple bracelets and hooped earrings (National Museum, Bangkok). During this period trade tribute was sent to the Chinese emperors of the Song dynasty (960–1279). Records from a small state situated near present-day Nakhon Si Thammarat, southern Thailand, list dyestuffs, blankets and floral textiles (Wong 1979). In exchange the Chinese sent silver, copper, rolls of silk, and sets of garments and accessories (Fraser-Lu 1988). Early twentieth-century court costumes from Keng Tung, Chiang Mai and Bangkok show a continuing taste for Chinese silks, embroideries and velvets, adapted to the local style of dress.

In AD 1238 the Tai expelled the Khmer and established their capital on the fertile central plains at Sukhothai. Evidence of costume style comes from stone carvings in temples. Women wear floral- or geometric-patterned sarongs wrapped around the body, one end passing between the legs to be fastened in a tie at the waist. They are portrayed bare-breasted and wear necklaces and bracelets. Men wear mid-calf-length trousers with a knee-length pleated sarong tied over the top. They are depicted wearing short-sleeved shirts with patterned borders at the neck and sleeve edge, and a pleated sash is worn over the top. Their head-dresses appear to be made of metal with decorative panels on the front. There is scant information on the colour and fabrics used, although in a letter written by the Chinese diplomat Chou Ta Kuan in 1296 it is recorded that 'the Siamese use delicately woven black silk to construct garments and Siam women can sew very well'. On the stone inscriptions at Sukhothai there is mention of a five-coloured cloth called *bencharongse* (see p. 27), which is also mentioned in diplomatic and trade records of

Classical court dancer, Bangkok. The costume consists of a bodice worn under a lined shawl, short at the front and long at the back, with a neck opening. The wrapped skirt is arranged in pleats at the front and held in place with a belt. A golden head-dress, bracelets and anklets complete the costume.

97

the thirteenth century (Chumbala 1985). The colours were red, white, green, yellow and black.

Situated to the south of Sukhothai, Ayuthya was the capital of Siam from 1350 to 1767 and during that time was an important centre for textile trade. Siamese royalty and high-ranking officials ordered printed cottons, *patolas* and brocaded silks from India. The court also ordered some weft *matmi* textiles from north-east Thailand and Cambodia, which were patterned in a similar fashion to the *patolas* imported from India. The court set strict dress codes for royalty, ministers and courtiers. Only the king and queen wore gold brocaded satins, while other consorts wore less elaborate brocades. Wives of ministers and royal servants were dressed in carefully graded qualities of fabric according to rank. Court jewellery and ritual items were lavish. Archaeological excavations at Wat Rat-

Detail of a stucco frieze portraying worshipping Buddhist disciples. Wat Mahathat, Sukhothai, 14th century.

burana (constructed 1424–48) uncovered golden head-dresses set with rubies and semi-precious stones, gold bracelets, rings and ritual objects (Pisit and Diskul 1978).

King Narai of Ayuthya (1656–88) started a fashion for foreign clothes when he ordered garments from France, but after his death taxes on imported goods were increased and the kingdom became less attractive to foreign investors and merchants. The Siamese were suspicious of French and British colonial expansion in the East and feared European interference in the country's internal affairs. In 1766 the Burmese again invaded Siam and a period of instability and famine followed, leading to a further decline in trade with the West.

Following the sacking of Ayuthya by the Burmese in 1767, the capital of Siam was moved to a new site on the Chao Phya river, at Bangkok. Built by King Rama I, the new city flourished; foreign traders settled there and a new era of expansion began. King Rama

Carved stone figure in a geometrically patterned loincloth, rolled and tucked at the waist. The figure also wears bracelets and anklets. Wat Ratburana, Ayuthya, 14th–15th centuries.

I allowed the importation of foreign textiles, although he imposed strict regulations on those who could wear them. Textiles woven or printed in India were prepared especially for the Siamese who sent patterns to be copied in India (see pp. 171–6). Often the imported woven textiles were then copied by skilled local weavers, which leaves the origin of some woven court textiles in doubt. Printed textiles remained an Indian trade good; the complex techniques of mordanting and dyeing were not mastered by the Siamese.

The decline in trade with the West continued until the reign of King Rama IV (1851–68), also known as King Mongkut. The king was anxious to modernise the kingdom and built railways, roads and schools and signed trade agreements with the West. In 1868 he was succeeded by his son, King Rama V (known as King Chulalongkorn). King Chulalongkorn made two world tours, in 1897 and 1907, and was photographed in Europe wearing fashionable Edwardian

Princess Ubon, daughter of Choa Kawilorot, Prince of Chiang Mai, wearing a traditional *phasin* with patterned hem border and a pleated sash, 1867. Pitt Rivers Museum.

The future King Rama VII (Prince Prajadhipok) dressed for the top-knot ceremony. Bangkok, c. 1900. Siam Society.

dress with a silk top hat, his courtiers wearing suits with bowlers or trilby hats. On his visit to Tsar Nicholas II of Russia the king was introduced to the fabulous creations of Carl Fabergé and became a regular customer, ordering jewellery and *objets d'art*.

With the re-establishment of diplomatic relations with the West, a sizeable foreign community was established in Bangkok. When the European ladies arrived in their fussy Edwardian clothes they were critical of their Siamese sisters in silk wraps and shoulder-sashes, although such elegant, simple outfits were obviously more suited to the humid climate. The Siamese ladies succumbed to Western fashions when they began to wear lacy blouses with leg-of-mutton sleeves, a style made fashionable by England's Queen Alexandra. Many of these blouses were ordered in Bangkok from newly opened European stores, and sales representatives made regular visits to the royal palace to fill orders from the ladies of the court, although some items were ordered directly from Europe. King Chulalongkorn's wife, Queen Patehrarintara, started the fashion for long strings of pearls and diamond necklaces, some of which were designed for her by Fabergé.

The ever-increasing decoration on the blouses and the opulent necklaces made the traditional silk shoulder-sash redundant, and it was replaced by a fine silk chiffon sash called a *prae sapai* (Chumbala 1985). Although Siamese ladies had adopted some Western fashions, they continued to wear the *pha chong kaben* wrap with the addition of white silk stockings and shoes. However, these Western fashions were not appropriate in the heat and humidity of Bangkok, and from accounts of life at court it appears that in the privacy of their apartments the royal ladies returned to more comfortable, traditional garments. The princesses from the north and north-east who married into the royal family of Bangkok often preferred to wear woven textiles from their home provinces.

On State occasions the king and his courtiers dressed in elaborate costumes, modelled on those worn at the court of Ayuthya. Lavish gold brocades and silks encrusted with semi-precious stones were worn with elaborate jewellery. One of the grandest occasions was the *kon chook* hair-cutting ceremony which marks the entry of a child into adulthood. The royal children who underwent the ritual were dressed in the most elaborate gold brocades and jewellery, some borrowed from the royal store, others commissioned from India, and some ordered from weavers in the provinces. In the textile collection of Princess Boonchiradorn Chutatuij (1897–1979), who was brought up in the royal household of Bangkok, there is a length of silk brocaded with gold thread, woven in Chiang Mai province, and a silk length brocaded in silver, woven by Madame Koon Na Champasak who was a renowned weaver from Ubon Ratchatani province (Chumbala 1985). These textiles were worn at important

A formal photograph of a Siamese provinicial governor wearing a pleated *pha chong kaben* with his Western clothes, 1924. Pitt Rivers Museum.

court ceremonies. Today, in north-east Thailand, highly skilled weavers such as Pa Payom from Roi Et take commissions for brocaded silks and *matmi*, which are worn by royalty and officials at court.

In Bangkok at the turn of the century the fashion for Western blouses continued, but the traditional *pha chong kaben* was replaced by the *phasin* skirt, which had always been a style worn in the north and north-east. In the 1920s the *phasin* was shortened to mid-calf, in keeping with the 'flapper' dresses of the West. With the revolution

in 1932, radical changes took place in government and society. Decrees were passed to impose European fashion on all levels of society. Men wore Western suits and hats, and women began to tailor their skirts, replacing the method of wrapping and folding which had always been the custom. Instead of adapting European fashions as they had done in the past, the people were now forced to copy slavishly.

In 1946, when King Bhumibol Adulyadej acceded to the throne, Western clothes and fabrics were still in demand, and his consort Queen Sirikit expressed concern for the future of traditional Thai dress and for the livelihoods of hand-weavers. Her Majesty undertook a study of costumes from the seventh century to the present, with assistance from fashion designers and costume historians. As a result of this research five outfits were chosen, for daytime and evening wear, all woven in Thai silk using traditional weaving patterns. They were received with great acclaim and were copied throughout the country. Each outfit was given a name and appropriate occasions were suggested for their use.

Thai ruan ton – casual daytime wear, consisting of a striped *phasin*, folded to the side, and a collarless blouse with three-quarter length sleeves.

A procession in Chiang Mai, north Thailand. The women are wearing a modern adaptation of traditional costume, with long-sleeved blouses and sashes co-ordinated with their *phasin*.

Thai chitralada – worn for formal daytime occasions. The *phasin* has a fold at the front and may be patterned. The blouse has a mandarin collar and full-length sleeves.

Thai amarin – worn for informal evening occasions. The *phasin* has a fold at the front and is woven of gold brocade or has gold brocade in the border. The blouse has a mandarin collar and is fastened at the front with jewelled buttons.

Thai borompimarn – worn for formal evening occasions. The *phasin* is woven of gold or silver brocade, with a decorated front pleat. The blouse fastens at the back and has a mandarin collar.

Thai chakri – worn on State occasions. The *phasin* is of heavy gold or silver brocade, pleated at the front. The blouse is cut like a bustier with a shoulder-sash worn over the top. A silver or gold belt is worn at the waist.

In 1976 Queen Sirikit set up SUPPORT, a foundation which sponsors Thai arts and crafts, hand-woven textiles being one of the main beneficiaries. Their continued promotion has kept indigenous weaving patterns in the public eye and set a fashion, especially for *matmi* silk and cottons. International designers have used Thai hand-woven textiles in their collections, and this has encouraged designers in the Thai fashion houses to do the same. Private companies such as the Jim Thompson Thai Silk Company assure the continued production and high quality of Thai silk.

An early history of costume in the rural areas of Thailand is more difficult to trace than at court. Travellers in the seventeenth century, like Thomas Samuel of the East India Company, saw the country more as a market for imported textiles from India and make no mention of local cloth in the list of possible exports. In 1587 a merchant from London, Ralph Fitch, reached Chiang Mai and wrote: 'I went from Pegu to Chiang Mai . . . The men are well set and strong with a cloth about them, bare-headed and bare-footed for in all these countries they wear no shoes' (Hudson 1965).

Outside the court centres there was little opportunity for travellers and traders to explore the country, especially during the eighteenth century when there were prolonged wars with Burma. However, by the nineteenth century diplomatic relations with the West had improved and foreigners were permitted to travel in the countryside. Their written accounts give a picture of the life and customs of the people. However, these accounts were written by government officials, foresters, engineers, missionaries and company agents, and their references to local costume and textile patterns are usually restricted to general impressions. One exception was the British Consul to Chiang Mai, Reginald Le May, who travelled extensively describing many aspects of local life, including costume. On his way north from Bangkok in 1913 he passed through Uttaradit, situated at the northern end of the central plains in the valley of the Nan river.

> As far as Utaradit [Uttaradit] the gradient is small, but after leaving that garrison town, the train goes up and up, winding slowly around the hillsides; on the one side are deep ravines, densely covered with jungle, on the other, towering above in sharp contrast, a mass of sheer rock . . . . At Ban Tan, just above Utaradit [Uttaradit], we reached the lowest outposts of the Lao people, and I was filled with admiration at a bevy of Lao beauties who had come down from their village to the station to see the wonderful train. They were dressed in the Lao 'Sin' or skirt . . . with a close fitting bodice above, and had their hair dressed in layers, rather like the coils of a snake, with a red flower gracefully worn at the side (Le May 1926).

Of Nan Province he wrote:

> Nan also produces, in rivalry to Chieng Mai [Chiang Mai], a large selection of beautiful silk and cotton skirts, by many considered the finest in Siam; and certainly the designs and colours chosen are in nearly every case both bold and pleasing. The Nan silk sin that I saw, which were made in the Palace, were of the finest quality. Also, in many another district may be found a type of cloth woven in designs peculiar to the locality (Le May 1926).

From the early eighteenth century the best visual sources for costume and textile history in the rural areas are Buddhist mural paint-

Detail of a painted border from a 19th-century mural painting, Wat Buak Khrok Luang, Chiang Mai province. Pendant patterns, both simple and complex, are used as border decoration in both pure and applied arts, including textiles.

ings. They decorate the walls of temples in villages and regional towns which were the centres for small princely states. Mural painters were commissioned by Buddhist monks and the laity. As most villagers were unable to read and write, the paintings were a means of explaining the life of the Buddha and Buddhist religious concepts. Before reaching the final stage of enlightenment the Buddha had many lives, including as a prince, a pauper and an aesthete. Hinayana Buddhism is practised in Thailand and according to its teachings scenes from everyday life are permitted with the religious. This gave artists an opportunity to set the stories of the Buddha's life in royal palaces, villages and the countryside, and to portray the people who lived in these settings. The murals of north Thailand portray costumes of the Tai Yuan and Tai Lue, hill-tribe groups, royalty, Siamese officials, soldiers, the Burmese and other visitors from abroad. The temple murals of north-east Thailand portray the costumes of the Tai Lao, Siamese officials, Siamese soldiers and hill-tribe groups. As travelling in north-east Thailand was difficult before the middle of this century, Western travellers were an unusual sight and their presence is rarely recorded in north-east temple murals.

The temples have murals with scenes of everyday village life, men and women labouring in the fields, ploughing with water-buffalo, planting and harvesting rice, women tending flowers and vegetables, preparing meals, spinning and weaving or trading in the market. The mural paintings of Ayuthya and Bangkok portray scenes of the life and customs of the royal court. In palace scenes princesses decked in gold jewellery recline on silk cushions surrounded by their attendants. The religious life of the people is portrayed in scenes of temple ceremonies, with monks officiating while villagers sit on floor mats, their hands joined in prayer. Of prime interest to the textile historian are scenes where weaving patterns on costumes and household textiles can be identified. These include supplementary-weft patterns, *matmi* (ikat) and patterns of plied yarns and stripes. Court costumes and household textiles often had gold thread in the supplementary-weft patterns, and these are reproduced in the murals using gold leaf. Imported brocades, silks and printed cottons from India can also be identified.

A number of murals were restored in the nineteenth and early twentieth centuries, for example, at Wat Phumin in Nan province. Restorers have sometimes retouched costumes in a contemporary style, so that women wear Western-style blouses whereas in the original paintings they would have been bare-breasted or worn shoulder-sashes. Men's thigh tattoos have been painted over and trousers substituted for loincloths. However, not all restoration has brought change, and many murals have been restored to their original state.

In traditional rural households the women of the family produce the clothing. Cloth is woven in rectangles which are folded and tucked around the body. Women's costume consists of an ankle-length tubular skirt, called a *phasin*, and a shoulder-sash, sometimes used as a wrapper over the breasts. The Tai Lue, who settled in Thailand from Sipsong Panna, southern China, wore a *phasin* with a cotton blouse. The blouses had a wrapover front fastened with ties at the side with colourful embroidery and trimmings. Tai Lue women also wear white cotton turbans. Village women tucked fresh flowers into their hair as decoration, while wealthy women wore gold necklaces, wide cylinders of gold in their ears, and bracelets, often studded with rubies and semi-precious stones. The elaborate earrings required large holes in the earlobe. Written accounts from the nineteenth century explain the method used to pierce the ears. A small wooden peg was inserted into the lobe and replaced at intervals with larger pegs until the hole was about an inch (2.5 cm) in diameter (Bock 1884, repr. 1986). Besides providing a hole big enough to insert large gold cylinders, the hole could also be used to carry a cheroot, or a small sprig of flowers.

In temple mural paintings and early photographs of rural Thailand women are often portrayed wearing a *phasin* with a sash. The sash is called a *pha sabai, pha biang* or *pha prae wa*, depending on the Tai ethnic group. Some sashes were woven in plain-weave silk or cotton; evidence from mural paintings suggests that blue, yellow, white or red were the preferred colours. In north-east Thailand the

Tai Lue lady wearing a turban, Ban Nong Bua, Nan province.

Girls in central Thai costume, 1862. The girl standing to the left wears a pleated silk sash, fashionable from the beginning of the 19th century. All three wear silk *pha chong kaben*. Pitt Rivers Museum.

sashes are often woven of white silk. The Phu Tai of north-east Thailand wear red silk sashes decorated with a brightly patterned supplementary weft.

The Siamese who settled in the north and north-east as administrators and traders continued to wear the *pha chong kaben* and had their hair cut short, easily distinguishing them from local women. Holt S. Hallet in 1889 commented on this difference in style:

> Amongst the Siamese the dress of the two sexes is exactly alike, but the women are shorter and more brazen-faced than the men and wear a love-look [sic] above each ear. Both have their hair cut short at the back and sides of the head, and wear it either swept back from the forehead or parted in the middle. It is very thick, coarse, and intensely black.

In the rural areas the most colourful and varied part of a woman's costume was her *phasin* skirt. Often each section is quite distinctive in pattern – for example, plain bands sewn to striped bands which

are sewn to multicoloured borders. The bands are woven using a variety of weaving techniques including *matmi*, supplementary weft, supplementary warp, tapestry weave and plain weave. The various patterns and the manner in which they are arranged establishes the ethnic affiliation of the wearer. Some of the more subtle distinctions, such as slight variation in pattern or dye colour, may indicate a particular district. Men's loincloths and sarongs are restricted to plaids, stripes and plied yarn patterns which make ethnic affiliation less discernible. However, the woven shoulder-sashes which they wear to the temple come in a variety of colours and patterns which are associated with individual ethnic groups.

The weavers in the villages claim that until about forty years ago it was possible to identify a woman's ethnic origin solely by the style of her *phasin*, and in some cases to specify the district where she lived. In north Thailand weaving patterns tended to be similar along river valleys which were the main means of communication before roads were built. However, variations in pattern and style could often be narrowed down to a region of a few square miles in particular valleys which were isolated from their neighbours. This evolution into distinctive styles came about as a result of isolation and was to end once roads and railways were built.

The master weaver Ba Sangda Bansiddhi of Chom Ton, Chiang Mai province, said that it was the custom among village weavers to gather silk moths in the wild and breed them at home to produce enough silk for a set of best clothes. A woman might weave only one silk set to last her lifetime. On ceremonial occasions many women wore cotton costumes containing brightly coloured patterns, often woven with brilliant yellow yarn which simulated the gold thread worn by the wealthy. The royal families of Chiang Mai and Nan regularly wore silk, decorated with gold thread, either produced locally or imported from north-east Thailand, Cambodia, China or India. These imported materials were adapted to local costume styles, and court *phasin* are sometimes a combination of locally woven fabric and imported cloth.

In the settled farming communities of rural Thailand men spend a great deal of their time working in the fields and tending farm animals. For this work they seem most comfortable in loose-legged cotton trousers or a simple plaid cotton sarong and an indigo cotton shirt, with a palm-leaf hat for protection against the sun. They also wear a length of plaid cotton, called a *pha koma*, which serves as a

Detail of a man's silk sarong, Si Sa Ket province. Each square contains a silk warp and plied weft yarns in varying colours which together create a shimmering plaid. White silk warp and weft stripes border and accentuate the colour of each square. Isan Culture Museum, Khon Kaen University.

Left A man in a plaid sarong and *pha koma* strolling in the village of Ban Hin Lad, Khon Kaen province.

waistband, a bathing wrap or a sweat-cloth. Around the village they can be seen relaxing in plaid sarongs with a *pha koma* worn as a shoulder-sash. To go to the temple they wear front-buttoned shirts, trousers or sarongs with a special *pha koma*, often woven of silk. Tai Lue men wear distinctive indigo shirts with hand-stitched patterns on the collars and shoulder-sashes with complex supplementary-weft patterns.

In north and north-east Thailand mural paintings and old photographs provide evidence of what was worn at court. In the paintings we see men in patterned *pha chong kaben* with waist-sashes, front-buttoned, mandarin-collared shirts and, occasionally, long-sleeved jackets or loose cloaks. Many of these *pha chong kaben* were imported

Right Detail of a temple mural painting, Wat Phumin, Nan province, showing a woman gently brushing the leg of her tattooed lover with the back of her hand.

from India; patterns were sent to be copied as the technique for painting, printing and mordanting cotton was not known in Siam. Those worn by members of the royal family were intricately patterned and stamped with gold leaf. In the eighteenth century the market in Siam was flooded with cheap Indian copies of these printed cottons which were affordable by many levels of society. In the mural paintings of Chiang Mai and Nan courtiers and servants are often portrayed in patterned *pha chong kaben* which are probably meant to portray these cheap Indian imports. Other murals portray men in plain or simple, checked and striped *pha chong kaben* woven locally.

Although men's costumes are generally less colourful than women's, in the old days their flamboyance and pride in their masculinity were expressed in the most stunning body tattoos which extended from above the waist to just below the knee. Some men chose to be tattooed on the chest and back too. The practice of tattooing was common in the Shan states of Burma, the Lanna kingdom, Isan and western Laos. The tattoos can be seen in temple mural paintings in north and north-east Thailand, and there are some elderly men living in the villages who are tattooed in the traditional way, although they no longer wear the scant loincloths which so beautifully displayed the patterns. Some Lanna princes and men of high rank were also tattooed; they can be seen in the mural paintings wearing brocaded silk or patterned cotton *pha chong kaben*, with tattoos just visible below their knees. Soldiers are portrayed riding elephants and horses into battle, their tattoos thought to provide protection against injury.

In the villages of north-east Thailand the old men say that a full set of leg tattoos from waist to knee took two days to complete and

Eighty-two-year-old man from Ban Hin Lad, Khon Kaen province, with tattooed thighs. There are few men still living who have such elaborate and extensive tattoos.

that they took opium to help withstand the pain. Even with opium some men were still unable to bear the ordeal and never completed a full set. Tattoo artists regularly toured the villages, and the men chose what they wanted from drawings or just asked for certain symbols. Tattooing was considered as a sign of a man's courage and was highly favoured by local women. One man of eighty-four said that when he was young no girl would consider marrying a man if he was not tattooed, which was termed as 'being made beautiful forever'. The following account by the traveller Carl Bock (1884, repr. 1986) describes the practice in the nineteenth century:

> The figures selected are much of the same in character in all cases though as only one colour – black – is used and as there are no special marks or signs to denote any particular rank –

beggar and king being equal in the hands of the professional tattooer – the exact pattern is left to the individual choice of the patient or the skill of the operator. The pigment is made from the smoke of burning lard, the soot from which is collected in earthenware pots and mixed with the bile of the wild bull, bear or pig, a little water being added to give it the proper consistency; once rubbed in the colour is indelible. Two kinds of instruments are employed, one being a sharp serrated plate, something resembling a grainer's comb and used for making the plain tracery, or 'stippling' and the other a kind of style made of a solid piece of steel with a sharp point, and longitudinal grooves for holding the paint. With this instrument the various figures are pricked into the skin.

The figures chosen for tattoos are characters in Tai mythology, some from the *Ramakien* (the *Ramayana*); the same figures can be seen in woven textiles, particularly ceremonial sashes and temple banners. The following list, adapted from Carl Bock, gives the figures used by tattoo artists:

1. The Rachasee. According to Tai legend the king of beasts who was born of two bears. He was the most beautiful and powerful of beasts and his effigy guards the entrance to many temples.
2. The Elephant. Associated with royalty, a white elephant is the Tai symbol of divinity.
3. Birds. These include the pigeon (Nok Gatap), the vulture (Nok Ring) and the heron (Nok Kapbua).
4. The Tiger (Seua). A representative of evil spirits but his image brings physical strength.
5. The Monkey (Ling). A symbol of longevity, it never dies but goes in old age to live in the clouds.
6. The Rat (Noo).
7. The Hoalaman (Hanuman). A mythical creature who features in the *Ramakien* stories.

By the end of the nineteenth century European dress became fashionable in the northern city of Chiang Mai. Narrow-legged trousers, Edwardian shirts, blouses, shoes and hats appear in photographs of the period. In north Thailand the new fashions were adopted by royalty, government officials and wealthy traders. Photographs taken in Chiang Mai in the late nineteenth century show officials wearing Edwardian jackets, boots, plus-fours, long socks and two-tone shoes. By the end of the nineteenth century formal menswear consisted of a mixture of Western and local fashions. A plain or patterned round-necked shirt with long or short sleeves was worn with a *pha chong kaben* and a sash or belt. Long white socks and leather shoes completed the outfit, although Western travellers recount that socks and shoes were reserved for

Chao Phraya Yomaraj and his family, *c.* 1900. The ladies wear Western-style blouses with *pha chong kaben*. Chao Phraya Yomaraj is dressed in uniform worn during the reign of King Chulalongkorn (Rama V). The white linen jacket worn by his son (standing left) was also fashionable at that time. Siam Society.

Far right A villager from Ban Na Ka, north-east Thailand, wearing a cotton *matmi phasin* and blue camisole top.

formal occasions (Hallet 1889). Head-coverings included bowler hats, pith helmets, caps and straw hats which are portrayed in both mural paintings and photographs. The ladies in the photographs of the time wear traditional *phasin* and high-necked lacy blouses with leg-of-mutton sleeves. This mixture of East and West did not please everyone. Carl Bock wrote from the north in 1882:

> A few Lao women are beginning to wear tight fitting jackets cut to the shape of the figure with equally tight fitting sleeves something after the style of the 'ladies jerseys' recently so fashionable in London and Paris and involving no small amount of labour to fit on and off being made not of elastic knitted work but of unyielding cotton or silk. But this innovation spoils the pleasing appearance of the women in their ordinary dress.

The villagers who remained isolated from the towns continued to wear their traditional woven costumes well into the twentieth century, although there is evidence that missionaries were able to persuade female converts and girls in their schools to cover their breasts

A village festival in Chiang Mai province. This team of dancers performs regularly, their costumes a modern interpretation of traditional dress.

Far right Men attending a Buddhist ceremony in the city of Chiang Mai. They wear indigo cotton shirts and loose-legged trousers with plaid waist-sashes. A temple banner can be seen in the background.

with a blouse (Hallet 1889). Communication in the rural areas began to improve slowly. The first major road from Lampang to Chiang Mai was completed in 1916, but it was not until after the Second World War that a road was opened between Bangkok and Chiang Mai. In the north-east dirt tracks and rivers were the only means of travel until the late 1940s.

However, exposure to Western-style dress reached the rural areas once roads were opened. Western fashions were copied by village dressmakers from magazines and newspapers. A new style of dress for women evolved, Western or Chinese blouses worn with the traditional *phasin* and a *pha sabai* over the blouse. Hairdressing salons opened in the urban and rural areas, and women had their hair bobbed or styled with a permanent wave. Village women wore blouses or camisoles while working in the fields, although they continued to wear *phasin*. In the last twenty years young people have adapted ethnic dress to their own style. At temple festivals girls are seen in *phasin* with traditional weaving patterns but cut like Western-style skirts. Jeans and trousers are now worn by women for field work, although a number continue to wear *phasin*. Some villages support teams of dancers who perform at temple festivals, and their costumes are an interesting mixture of traditional costume and Western dress. In the villages men continue to wear practical clothes for agricultural work; indigo cotton trousers cut in a loose Chinese style or mid-calf-length trousers with a low crotch called *tieo sado* (Cheesman 1987). A long- or short-sleeved indigo shirt completes the outfit. On formal occasions a plaid *pha koma* or patterned *pha chet* shoulder-sash is worn over the shirt. Each Tai ethnic group retains elements of its individual costumes and weaving patterns for ceremonial dress.

116

6

CEREMONIAL AND HOUSEHOLD TEXTILES

The people of Thailand are Buddhist, although some also observe traditions which are animist in origin. In the Buddhist cosmology there are innumerable worlds and star galaxies. Each world system has its own sun, moon and earth containing continents and oceans with a mountain, Mount Meru, in the centre and heavens above the mountain. These world systems are divided into three main categories – Kama Loka, Rupa Loka and Arupa Loka. Kama Loka is the plane of existence most relevant to the lives of the villagers of Thailand. It is divided into eleven worlds, six are heavens inhabited by gods, four are worlds inhabited by humans, animals, ghosts and demons, and the last is the world of hell. The heavens are inhabited by the god Indra, musicians and singers, the world guardians and *nagas* (serpents) who have the status of demi-gods. In one of the heavens resides the Bodhisattva (Buddha-to-be) who is waiting to come down into the world of men as the next Buddha and saviour. The heaven of the Bodhisattva is regarded as the most satisfying; in it grows a tree which produces fruits of gold, silver and jewels that satisfy all desires. The heavens and hell of the Buddhist cosmology are portrayed in the mural paintings which decorate the walls of many Thai temples. Patterns representing creatures and objects from the Buddhist cosmology are also woven in Thai ceremonial textiles and

Detail of a ceremonial cloth (possibly a banner), San Pathong, Chiang Mai province. The warp is hand-spun cotton, and the weft has alternating bands of undyed and yellow cotton, woven in plain weave. The supplementary-weft pattern contains elephants, horses, men on horseback and temples with Buddha images.

include the tree which produces gold and silver jewels, *nagas, rach-asee*, elephants, monkeys, birds and various mythical animals.

It is a Buddhist tradition that the laity support monks and novices by looking after their temporal needs. Every morning, at dawn, the monks set out with their begging bowls to collect food from the villagers, who wait on the threshold of their houses with an offering of rice, or a simple vegetable dish, which they ladle into the monks' bowls. In north-east Thailand a small procession often sets out down the narrow lanes to give the monks at the local monastery their pre-noon meal. The laity also provide clothing and household linen, which in some rural areas is hand-woven. These textiles may be donated by individuals or by groups of devotees during festivals – for example, Bun Kathin, when gifts are presented to the monks on a decorated palanquin.

Weaving textiles for the monks is an important task for women, especially if a male relative is about to enter the monastery. To

The Abbot of the temple of Wat Po Ngam, Khon Kaen province, with Acharn Suriya Smutkupt, inspecting a temple banner woven by the women of the village.

become a monk oneself, or have a son ordained, is one of the most important merit-making acts, bringing honour to the family. If a man is to be ordained, his mother, sisters or aunts will weave his robes and bed-linen, although today one sees more and more plastic-wrapped packets of machine-woven textiles at the presentation ceremonies. It is in the rural areas of north-east Thailand where women still routinely weave for the monks.

At the time of religious festivals woven banners, called *pha tung*, are part of the decorations hung inside the temples, and on Bun Phrawees (a major Buddhist festival) they are hoisted on bamboo poles set up in the temple grounds. Some woven banners are carried in religious processions, although most of these are painted on

Detail of a silk and cotton blanket, Mukdahan province, worn by a novice monk during the ordination procession. The warp is arranged in black, green and red bands with a supplementary warp of white and gold silk. The weft is black cotton. Photo Kim Retka.

Indigo blue cotton shoulder-bag, made for a monk, lined with plain cotton and decorated with tassels of two-ply, imported yarn.

cotton. There are also Tai Lue ceremonies associated with ancestor worship and funeral rites, when banners are hoisted on long bamboo poles, not always in the temple grounds. Because of the heat, high humidity and damage from insects, banners tend to have a short life and weavers have to replace them every three to five years. Discussions take place with the abbot and senior monks about the size and patterns, which include religious symbols common to Buddhist art throughout Asia. The monks appear to be well-informed about the level of weaving skills among women: they say the work is allocated according to ability, complex patterns being assigned to the most skilled women. After the religious ceremonies are over the woven banners are rolled up and stored in the temple, under the supervision of the monks.

Textiles for monks

Buddhist monks are recognised by their saffron robes which have three components – a sarong, a shoulder-sash and an outer robe long enough to envelop the whole body. The correct colour for robes was described as a dull yellow-brown, as laid down in the regulations from the monks' disciplinary code book (Suvatabandhu 1964). Today most robes are made from factory-processed cotton and dyed with aniline dyes, although in the rural areas of north-east Thailand women continue to weave robes, sometimes made of local silk. It was also the custom to weave a silk blanket which was worn by a novice during his procession to the monastery for ordination. During the Lenten season monks wear white cotton robes for ritual bathing. These were hand-spun and hand-woven in the villages but today most are of commercially produced cotton.

A monk's needs are very simple – a set of robes, some bed-linen, pillows and a bag to carry a few bare essentials when visiting other monasteries. The bed-linen today will probably be plain cotton sheets and blankets, but in former times sheets and blankets were woven with special patterns reserved for the religious (Henrikson 1978). The shoulder-bags are usually woven in plain weave and dyed the same colour as the monks' robes, although in some villages weavers make decorative bags in bright colours. There is disagreement among weavers about the suitability of these coloured bags, most women saying that bags should be plain and undecorated, others approving of brighter colours.

Temple banners

Before major Buddhist festivals villagers spend days in preparation, decorating the temples with woven banners, paper flags, plants and flowers. Each festival brings special requirements. For Bun Kathin a wooden palanquin is decorated with banana stems and flowers, and banners are brought out of store to be carried in procession to

Detail of a ceremonial banner, Ban Dong Phong, Khon Kaen province. The panel illustrated contains supplementary-weft patterns of elephants, horses and riders and religious offering bowls, woven in black and red silk. Below these patterns are weft stripes of pink, black, tan and yellow silk. The warp fringe has not been cut and is still attached to the end threads of the previous warp. Smithsonian, Institution, Washington, DC (photographer Victor Krantz). 206.5 × 21 in (525 × 53 cm).

the temple. For Bun Phrawees flag poles are sunk in the ground and large woven banners are hung from them; inside the temple smaller woven banners and painted flags are hung from the ceiling.

The following nineteenth-century account by Carl Bock (1884, repr. 1986) describes a decorated temple compound:

In front of the Wat is a tall flagstaff surmounted by a figure of a bird, representing the sacred goose. These flagstaves are to be seen in every temple ground with a number of streamers or flags (*tungs*) and are often useful as landmarks, for temples built near the rivers are often hidden from view by the thick forest and the flagstaves are purposely made very tall for the purpose of directing the traveller to the house of prayer.

In 1883 Bock visited a temple on Doi Suthep, a mountain overlooking the Chiang Mai valley in north Thailand:

> In the centre of the temple grounds towering above the tree tops was a tall prachedee, heavily gilt, like a temple itself and glistening in the brilliant sunlight against the dark background of the surrounding forest, while 'tungs' or flags innumerable floated gaily from flagstaves placed at every few yards and from every projection on the sacred edifices from which it was possible to suspend them.

The banners flown in temple grounds may be up to 20 ft (6 m) in length and are often woven by a team of weavers who choose the patterns with the local monks. Sometimes there is an addition to the usual Buddhist symbols of stupas, temples, elephants and religious offering bowls – for example, the name of the temple where the banner is to be flown. Woven with a cotton or silk ground weave, the banners have supplementary-weft patterns in a panel at the bottom or arranged at intervals throughout. Also inserted at intervals in the weft are sets of flat bamboo sticks which help keep the banners stiff when they are flying. The sticks extend from selvage to selvage or are arranged in cut patterns of religious images, such as stupas, temples, elephants and ceremonial offering bowls. Occasionally a banner will have the same patterns woven in the supplementary weft as are cut in the bamboo sticks. Each banner has a warp fringe at the base, tied with silver and metal bells, rods of bamboo, coloured yarn and paper streamers. When the banners are flying the metal bells tinkle in the breeze, and the decorative paper and yarn shine and rustle in the tropical light.

The tradition of weaving temple banners is still common in Nan province and parts of north-east Thailand but seems to have ceased in the Chiang Mai valley, where many have been sold to dealers or cut into sections and sold to tourists.

The Tai Lue hold a special memorial ceremony in the New Year, two days after Songkran, the water festival, when they pay tribute to their ancestor spirits. White banners, the colour associated with death, are flown on long poles in the temple grounds. Once every three years a grand memorial ceremony to the ancestor spirits is held. Elderly weavers said that in the old days the banners were woven in white cotton, although today they are decorated with a supplementary weft of coloured yarns.

The Tai Lue believe that when a person dies the spirit is assisted to heaven on the upward spiralling motion of a banner as it spins in the breeze on a long bamboo flag pole. If a villager dies from

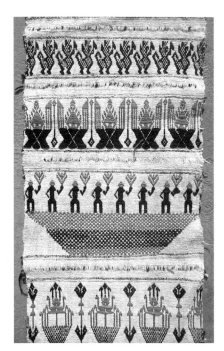

Detail of a ceremonial banner, Nan province. The warp and weft are plain, hand-spun cotton. The supplementary weft of reddish-brown and black cotton is woven in patterns of birds, religious offering bowls and a ship with men aboard holding tree branches, perhaps symbolising the Buddhist tree with fruits which satisfy all human desires.
67 × 10.5 in (170 × 27 cm).

natural causes, the banner will be predominantly white cotton with a coloured supplementary weft. An old lady from Nan province had been told by her father, who was of Laotian descent, that when he was a young man and there was a death in his village a group of women would quickly assemble to weave a banner. They worked as a team, rising early in the morning, spinning the yarn, preparing the warp and weft, and completing the weaving. The banner was woven in white cotton with white supplementary-weft yarns. Helping with the task was a way of making merit, and after it was flown for the spirit of the deceased it was presented to the temple.

White banners are associated with death by natural causes, but if there is death by accident the banner must be woven in red cotton and may include a supplementary weft of multicoloured yarns. The banner is taken to the scene of the accident where it is hoisted on a bamboo flag pole. Today, when car accidents are a common cause of death, these banners may sometimes be found at the side of the road. Tai Lue banners may be stored in the local temple but in some villages are kept in the house of the head man. This suggests that although flown in Buddhist rites they may also have secular significance.

As part of the preparation for the festival of Bun Phrawees, women put up gaily coloured flags made of paper, yarn and bamboo. These flags, like tiered spiders' webs, are associated with Phraa Uppakrut, the protector of the village and bringer of rains. The flags are said to be associated with the natural world and are hung inside the temple with other plant and floral decorations and are freshly made each Bun Phrawees festival.

The Tai Lue and Tai Lao weave banners up to 6 ft (1.8 m) long which are hung inside their temples, usually in the vicinity of the Buddha image. They contain a complex mixture of woven images, some common to the Buddhist art of Asia, others associated with Tai legends, many occurring also in other ceremonial textiles, like the *pha chet*.

The origin of Tai Lue banners can be traced to Sipsong Panna, southern China, where the styles are similar – an undyed cotton ground weave with supplementary-weft patterns in brown, red, or black cotton, often with a plaited warp fringe. The patterns contain images of temples, religious offering bowls, horses, elephants and mythical birds. Some also include ship patterns, with men standing on deck holding branches, perhaps meant to represent the gold and silver tree of the Buddhist Yunita heaven, a tree believed to satisfy all earthly desires. Their similarity with Sumatran ship cloths has been discussed in Chapter 1. The banners also contain woven images of birds, elephants and *rachasee*, seen also in thigh tattoos (see Chapter 5). There are narrow spaces at intervals in the cotton weft for the insertion of individual bamboo sticks, which help keep

Detail of a ceremonial banner, Khon Kaen province. The warp and weft are plain cotton. There is a supplementary-weft pattern of birds and elephants woven in blue, red, tan and orange cotton.

the banners stiff. The borders contain pendant patterns like those seen around temple mural paintings and stencilled in gold on temple doors, window shutters and support pillars. These pendant patterns also occur in the borders of printed textiles (see Chapter 1).

Tai Lao banners also contain images associated with Buddhism and Tai legends, but the weaving patterns have a definite Laotian style. The banners consist of a cotton ground weave with supplementary-weft patterns in multicoloured cotton and have a plain warp fringe. Patterns include Laotian-style temples and offering bowls, birds, elephants and horses.

Animist textiles

The Tai people are Buddhist but also follow some animist traditions (see Chapter 2). They perform rituals to appease the spirits of their ancestors, the guardian spirits of the home and compound, and the spirits of the fields, swamps and forests. Simple, plain, cotton cloths, painted or drawn with magical symbols, were displayed during animist rites. Some which were carried into battle as protection were printed with symbols believed to ward off injury from arrows, bullets, knives, swords and stones from sling shots; others were thought to offer protection from illness.

Household textiles

In a traditional Thai household the women of the family weave all the items required to make the family comfortable at home. They make mattresses, bed-linen and mosquito-nets, as well as triangular pillows which support the back while sitting on the floor and square pillows used for sleeping. These household textiles are exchanged at important family occasions such as weddings and house blessings, and are presented to the monks at temple ceremonies. In former times there was a code for choosing patterns, some woven only for monks, some for individuals within the family, and others for guests; today these distinctions are no longer upheld.

The beauty of a Thai house is in its coolness and simplicity. Traditional houses were built on stilts and constructed of teak with polished floors and elegant teak interiors, although the very poor live in dwellings of bamboo matting and rice thatch, and today concrete pillars and brick walls are common materials for new housing, indicating the scarcity of wood. Shoes are always removed at the bottom of the stairway before entering the house: the cool smooth floor is as welcoming as the traditional *wai* greeting, two hands brought together in front of a slightly bowed head. The main living space, where meals are served and guests entertained, is provided by a covered verandah. Woven reed mats are laid out on shiny teak floors, with colourful triangular cushions to support the back. Simple wooden cupboards store family items; some flowers and decorations are displayed on shelves; and a portrait of the King and Queen of Thailand occupies a prominent position. To pass into the inner room one steps over a raised threshold providing a safeguard against evil spirits, which travel close to the ground. The inner room may be divided into separate sleeping-quarters with partitions, or be one large bedroom. The room is very adaptable as furniture is portable: the bed consists of a lightweight mattress which folds up, concertina fashion, and is stored when not in use. The mattress cover is made of indigo-dyed cotton, and the filling is kapok which is harvested locally from the kapok tree, *Ceiba pentandra*. The cover has a decorative woven border which is seen when the mattress is folded; many also have a decorated central panel, woven separately from the indigo cover and then stitched to it.

The nineteenth-century traveller Carl Bock (1844, repr. 1986) described the preparation of his bed when he visited a Thai dignitary:

> His wife I observed quietly spoke to two of the servants who at once set to work to prepare a bed for me in the corner of the room. This was neither a long or a costly operation, a couple of mats with pillows were laid on the floor and a cotton curtain hung round as a screen and I was without ceremony informed that my sleeping quarters were already at my service . . . of bedsteads there are none, the people sleeping on home made mattresses stuffed with cotton wool and surrounded by a mosquito curtain.

Bed sheets

When the mattress is laid out for the night it is covered with a bed sheet, called a *pha lop*. Bed sheets are woven in plain-weave cotton with a decorative supplementary-weft pattern, either in a border or

Detail of a cotton bed sheet, Nan province. Plain-weave cotton for two-thirds of the length, then decorated with a red cotton supplementary weft of hooks, diamonds and floral patterns and a frieze of black cotton horses.

Detail of a bridal bed sheet, Phichit province. Plain cotton warp and weft with a supplementary weft. The top section contains diamonds, hooks, waves and floral patterns woven in yellow, green, blue and tan silk. The lower section has an indigo cotton supplementary weft woven with diamonds, hooks, plant and floral motifs.

Detail of a bridal bed sheet, Phichit province. Plain hand-spun cotton warp and weft with a supplementary weft. The top section has rows of geometric patterns, bordered by a hook motif, woven in red, lilac, green and yellow silk. The lower section has an indigo cotton supplementary weft woven with hooks, triangles and floral patterns.

extending throughout the length. They are woven in two bands, sewn together at the selvage. When a girl marries, a decorated sheet containing supplementary-weft patterns with multicoloured yarns in the borders is woven for the marriage bed. There is evidence in the mural paintings that members of the royal family slept on patterned sheets edged with gold thread.

Blankets

Thailand has a tropical climate and at night, in most parts of the country, only a lightweight cotton blanket, called a *pha hom*, is

127

Detail of a cotton blanket, Nan province. The warp and weft contain bands of red, white and black cotton woven in a diamond float weave.

Far right and page 130 Details of cotton blankets, Khon Kaen province. Plain white cotton warp, the weft contains geometric patterns in black and white cotton. Isan Culture Museum, Khon Kaen University.

required to keep warm. However, in the highlands, during the cool season, the temperature can drop to freezing-point and then a thicker blanket is needed to keep warm during the day and at night. Regular lightweight blankets are woven in two lengths and sewn together along the selvage; they are made to cover a Thai-style mattress with an overlap. For the cool season the blanket is woven double the normal length and folded to give two layers, or an extra cotton lining is added to the regular lightweight blanket. Blankets are woven in plain- or float-weave patterns in plaids and stripes. Some have supplementary-weft patterns in geometric designs, woven in red, black or blue cotton. Traditionally the cotton was home-grown and hand-spun; indigo plants, shellac and ebony berries were used to make the dyes. In recent years these have been replaced by aniline dyes, and the cotton yarn is purchased in skeins from local village markets. However, in some regions of north-east Thailand and in Nan province, north Thailand, some women continue to make blankets using hand-spun, indigenous cotton.

Pillows

In rural Thailand villagers sit on the floor on woven mats, with brightly coloured cushions, called *maun*, to rest their backs and

128

Right A Buddhist shrine placed at the head of the bed. The Buddha image is standing on a woven ceremonial cloth. Water bottles, a fan and rectangular bed pillows can also be seen. Siam Society.

arms. When seated correctly the feet are tucked neatly to one side, never pointing at another person (considered to be ill-mannered), and the back is supported with a cushion. The following nineteenth-century account by Carl Bock (1884, repr. 1986) describes the seating arrangements in a wealthy Thai house:

> The best mats are edged with a red border and the cushions which are either oblong or three sided have their ends embroidered in silk or gold. When a visitor enters a mat is spread on the floor, with a cushion either behind to lean against, or at the side as a support to the arm – the quality of the cushions and mats selected depending entirely upon the rank of the visitor. The Chows [rulers] have, as a rule a table and a few chairs but seldom use the latter except when visited by 'distinguished strangers' when they look very uncomfortable as they sit cross legged on the seat.

The pillows for reclining are triangular in shape and densely packed with kapok to create a firm support for the back. For sleeping the pillows are narrow and oblong in shape, and not so densely packed. Pillows have bright covers, woven in narrow bands of plain and patterned silk or cotton sewn together along the selvage. Usually the number of bands needed to make a cover is between eight and ten, often arranged in pairs each side of a central band. Some bands are plain, some have simple stripes, others have continuous supplementary-weft patterns, called *khit maun*, of temples, elephants, religious offering bowls, flowers, animals, plants and abstract geometric patterns. In traditional Thai households individual pillows were woven for members of the family, for guests,

131

relatives and for the monks. Each pillow contained woven patterns deemed suitable to the user. For presentation to the monks pillows had patterns with religious significance; for family and friends the patterns were secular. The table below, compiled by Vimolphan Peetatawatchai (1973), lists pillow patterns and their relevant use:

Khit Kor Dork Kid (yellow flower) for presentation to the monks at ordination ceremonies.

Khit Maeng Ngao (insect) for household guests.

Khit Garb Yai for presentation to elders as a sign of respect.

Khit Garb Noi for a prospective son-in-law.

Khit Tapao Hlong Gaw (boat) for ordination ceremonies.

Khit Dork Kaeow (white flower) for presentation to elders as a sign of respect.

Khit Kor (hook design) for household guests.

Khit Dork Soey (beautiful flower) for a prospective son-in-law.

Khit Charng (elephant) for presentations to the monks or to commemorate a house blessing.

Khit Ngu Hluam (python) for household guests.

Khit Dork Chan (yellow flower) for Songkran, the water festival.

Khit Marg Mo for household use.

Khit Dork Peng (banana-leaf offering dish) for pillows presented to the monks at merit-making ceremonies.

Khit Maeng Ngord (scorpion) for household use.

Khit Oeng (frog) for friends and relatives.

Khit Kan Kra Hyong (bowl for temple flowers) for religious presentations.

A collection of patterned bands from north-east Thailand used in the making of pillow covers. Center for Northeastern Thai Art and Culture, Maha Sarakham University. Photo Gill Boardman.

7

$\diamond$

TEXTILES

OF NORTH

THAILAND

Temple mural painting, Wat Nong Bua, Nan province, depicting a Tai Lue lady wearing a red turban, a red flowing shoulder-sash lined in blue and a Nan-style *phasin*. The hem-border pattern is no longer visible as the paint has peeled from the surface.

North Thailand has a landscape of mountains and fertile valleys where the Tai have settled over many centuries, cultivating rice as their main food, the women weaving textiles for clothing and household use. During the many years of war with Burma groups of Tai fled from the large river valleys of Chiang Mai and Nan into remote valleys where they were safe from invading armies. Others were forcibly settled to repopulate areas which were decimated as a result of war. The environment was suited to textile production: women grew dyes such as indigo, along the fertile river banks, or gathered dye ingredients from the forests; they also had an ample supply of river water for dyeing and processing yarn. The main fibre grown for clothing was cotton, although silk cocoons were gathered from the wild in small amounts to produce yarn to weave a costume kept for special occasions.

The main ethnic group living in Chiang Mai province are the Tai Yuan, whose ancestors have lived in the area since before the founding of the Lanna kingdom in the thirteenth century. There are also Tai Lue who were forcibly settled in the nineteenth century and, at various times in history, Burmese from the Shan states who came to work in the teak-logging camps.

The *phasin* of Chiang Mai province is admired throughout the north; in neighbouring Burma the patterns were copied by Burmese weavers who called their *lungyi* skirts 'Chiang Mais' (verbal communication with Mrs N. K. Narayanan). Complex in construction, the *phasin* is made up of four separately woven bands sewn together along the selvage with a decorative stitch. The waistband is distinguishable from the hem, as according to Buddhist teaching the feet are considered unclean and the waistband should never, by

135

Right and page 137 A collection of hem borders, *teen jok*, chosen to illustrate the variety of patterns woven in Chiang Mai province. The multicoloured silk and cotton yarns are woven as discontinuous supplementary weft between rows of ground weave. The patterns are picked using the fingers or with the aid of a porcupine quill, the weaver working with the reverse side of the pattern facing her. The *jok* may be densely or loosely woven and the ply of the yarn may vary from very fine to thick ply. This gives immense variety to the character of each piece, from refined and delicate to a robust, heavier look.

Pages 138–9 Detail of a *phasin*, Chiang Mai province. The main panel contains warp stripes of black, green, yellow and purple cotton interspersed with white and red plied yarns. The weft is black cotton. The hem border has a decorative silk *jok* composed of geometric patterns and a bird motif. The pattern also contains gold and silver thread. There is a band of red cotton woven in plain weave at the base.

mistake, be reversed and worn near the feet (verbal communication with Acharn Suriya Smutkupt). The waistband, called a *hua*, is made of two strips of cotton, one undyed, the other woven of red or brown cotton, the two sewn together at the selvage with a simple running stitch to form a band 10–14 in (25–35.6 cm) deep. The *phasin* is gathered or folded into a pleat at the front and secured with a tuck. The hem band is usually made of cotton which does not slip, but if silk is used then a silver or metal belt or a sash is worn. The waistband is sewn to the central panel of the *phasin* with a simple running stitch or a decorative stitch in brightly coloured yarn.

The central panel called a *sin* is the widest of the four bands. In Chiang Mai province the most common patterns are sets of coloured stripes worn horizontally around the body. The stripes are prepared in the warp in a variety of widths and colours and include rows of plied yarns, called *da moo* in northern dialect. The weavers use varying thicknesses of spun yarn adding further variety to the overall look of the pattern. In the Chom Ton valley, to the south west of Chiang Mai, the weavers produce an indigo cotton *sin*, called *pha*

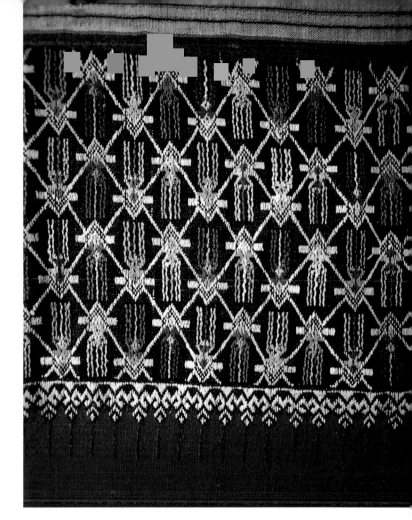

The hem border, *teen jok*, woven in silver thread, of a court *phasin* probably worn by a Chiang Mai princess.

hom uan in northern dialect. The pattern is made up of alternating bands of thick- and thin-ply indigo cotton in the warp and the same thick- and thin-ply bands in the weft, creating a semi-transparent cloth, often worn with a petticoat. In the court of Chiang Mai the ladies wore striped silk bands in the central panel of their *phasin*. The silk was produced locally or the yarn was imported from north-east Thailand, China or India. The central panel measures 20–24 (50–60 cm) in length, and the lower selvage is hand-sewn to the hem band with a decorative running stitch.

The hem band, called a *teen*, is a wide band of red, brown, black or blue cotton woven in plain weave. The hem reaches to the ankle and is often stained with the mud and dust of rice fields and dirt tracks; when it becomes worn it is replaced by a new band of plain cotton. On special occasions the plain band is replaced by a band of brightly coloured silk or cotton woven in a discontinuous supplementary-weft pattern called *jok*. The arrangement of the pat-

Detail of a *phasin*, Keng Tung, Burma. The hem band has panels of brocaded silk, bordered by silver and mother-of-pearl sequins and woven bands of silver and gold thread.

terns is complex: there is a top section of *jok* and closest to the feet a band woven in plain weave. The two sections are linked in the weft with a brocaded pattern and together form a band 10–15 in (25–38 cm) in length. *Jok* is woven in silk or cotton in a variety of colours and patterns, including stylised birds, plants and flowers and abstract patterns of squares, diamonds, hooks, hexagons and zigzags, and may contain gold and silver thread. It is a symbol of status – the wealthier the family the more silk, gold and silver thread are used. *Jok* is sometimes woven in brilliant yellow cotton, possibly an attempt by village weavers to imitate the golden thread worn by the wealthy.

Lanna, Keng Tung and Sipsong Panna

Keng Tung was the largest and most easterly of the Shan states of Burma and shared borders with Sipsong Panna, Lanna and Laos. From the thirteenth to the eighteenth centuries Keng Tung was part of the Lanna kingdom, and in the nineteenth century its sovereignty was disputed between Lanna and Burma. The princely states of Lanna engaged in skirmishes with Shan rulers until the end of the nineteenth century when the territory was finally recognised as part of Burma. The Tai of Keng Tung speak a dialect similar to northern Tai and have many cultural similarities, which are also shared by the Tai of Sipsong Panna. Their costumes have common design elements: the *phasin* of Keng Tung, Sipsong Panna and Lanna are similar in structure, with three sections of waistband, horizontally striped central panel and hem band. The Tai of Sipsong Panna and Keng Tung were excellent silversmiths and crafted silver sequins for their costumes. They were fond of Chinese embroidery silks and European velvet which they incorporated with their own woven panels.

Nan province

Nan province lies to the east of the Chiang Mai valley, separated by a range of small mountains. The Nan river, on which the town of Nan is situated, flows south through a wide fertile valley with tributaries from small valleys joining the main river. The town of Nan was once the capital of a princely state established in the thirteenth century. At various times in its history the state owed allegiance to the princes of Chiang Mai or came under the sway of the Burmese; it was not until 1931 that control moved to Bangkok. The largest Tai group living in the Nan valley are Tai Lue. Of Sino Tai origin, they migrated from Sipsong Panna, southern China, and in the last 200 years have settled in the Nan valley. There is a stone memorial in a village near Nan which was erected in memory of a prince who led one of the migrations. Some Tai Lue were forcibly settled in Lanna to repopulate areas devastated by wars with Burma.

The fertile valleys provide excellent rice harvests and secondary vegetable crops; the Tai Lue rear cotton as a secondary crop and in some areas use vegetable dyes. The weavers say there is no tradition of sericulture – they bartered for silk with the Tai Lao across the Mekong river (now part of Laos). As in the court of Chiang Mai, the royal family wore silk costumes decorated with silver and gold thread, often woven in the palace. Nan was famous for the skill of its weavers and the beauty of the patterns they produced. These complex costumes evolved as a result of the influx of Tai immigrant weavers from Sipsong Panna and their interaction with other Tai ethnic groups.

The Nan *phasin* is usually constructed of two main sections – a cotton waistband and a main panel with the weaving patterns arranged in the central section, continuing with plain bands at the hem. The central panel contains the most complex and colourful patterns using a variety of techniques, including weft *matmi*, tap-

Detail of a *phasin*, Nan province. The main panel of black and purple cotton is decorated with a supplementary weft of silver thread in a hand-picked geometric and *dork picun* (a small Thai flower) pattern. The silver thread was made of finely beaten silver wrapped around a silk core.

Far right Detail of the central panel of a cotton *phasin*, Nan province. Bands of blue and white and purple and white *matmi*, alternating with narrow cotton bands.

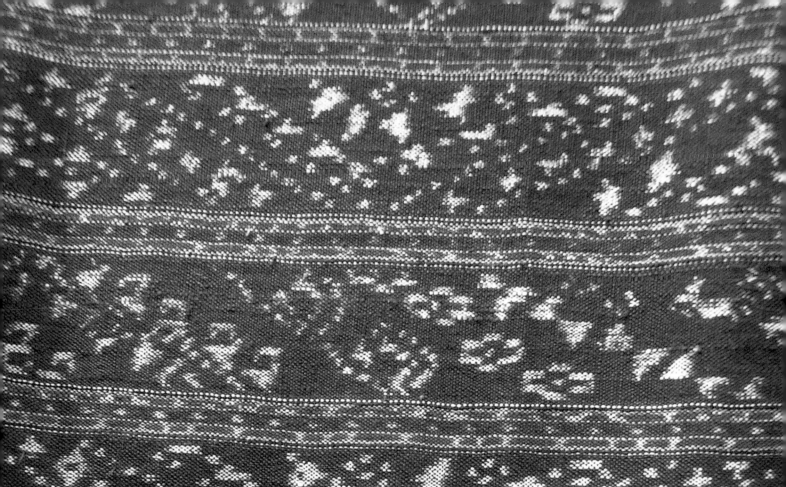

Right Detail of the central panel of a *phasin* from the court at Nan, possibly woven in the palace. Silk with weft stripes interspersed with rows of plied yarns. There is a fine supplementary-weft pattern in grey, black, yellow, pink and pale green silk.

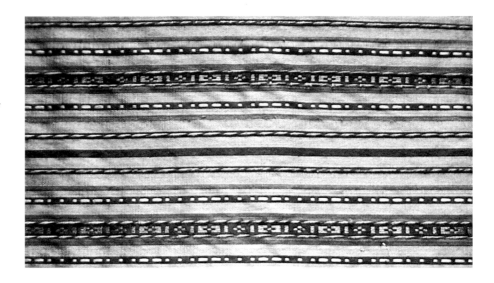

Detail of a *pha chet*, San Pathong, north Thailand. Plain hand-spun cotton warp and weft. Each end-panel is decorated with a reddish-brown and black cotton supplementary weft of ceremonial offering bowls, horses with riders, birds, frogs, elephants and *rachasee*.

Left Detail of the central panel of a cotton *phasin*, Nan province. Red and white cotton *matmi*, alternating with bands of supplementary weft woven in white, black, red and yellow cotton.

estry weave and supplementary weft. *Matmi* is said to be a technique which the Tai Lue learnt from the Tai Lao (verbal communication with Patricia Cheesman). The Nan *phasin* is usually woven in cotton; silk was reserved for special occasions and worn by the royal family of Nan. The royal *phasin* often have patterned hem borders of *jok*, similar to those woven in Chiang Mai province. The mural paintings of Wat Phumin and Wat Nong Bua provide ample evidence of the many patterns and styles of *phasin* worn in this region.

The *pha chet*

In north Thailand Tai Lue men wear a special shoulder-sash, called a *pha chet*, when they attend temple ceremonies. The sash is woven in hand-spun, undyed cotton with a supplementary weft. The patterns in the weft contain animal symbols which are found in tattoo patterns. Some include ships and bird motifs, also seen in the ship cloths of Sumatra. The woven borders are similar in pattern to those seen on stencilled temple pillars and wall friezes and as borders around temple mural paintings.

In rural Thailand villagers chew a preparation of areca palm nut, lime and tree bark, which stains the mouth red, and the *pha chet noi* is a small cloth which was used to wipe the juice from the mouth. In most cases the colours and patterns are similar to those of the *pha chet*, although for court use the cloths were often imported.

Wat Phra That Lampang Luang

Wat Phra That Lampang Luang is a sixteenth-century wooden temple with elaborately carved eaves and teak pillars. The site on which the temple stands was once part of a fortressed city built more than 1,000 years ago. The temple murals, which are painted on interior wood panels, are dated by Thai scholars as early eighteenth century (Simatrang 1983), although it is possible that these murals

Detail of a small imported cloth, *pha chet noi*, from the court of Chiang Mai, used to wipe betel-nut juice from the mouth. The central panel is cotton, covered in black lacquer, and the red silk end-borders are patterned with mirror embroidery. (See illustrations on pp. 11, 105.)

Far right Temple mural painting, Wat Buak Khrok Luang, Chiang Mai province, depicting Prince Siddhartha leaving his wife and child in the royal palace to enter an ascetic life. The prince wears a golden pagoda-style head-dress, a long-sleeved jacket with winged epaulettes trimmed with gold, and a red and gold waist-sash. Court attendants in Lanna costume are seen asleep in the foreground. In the background are large, floral-patterned textiles, used as room-dividers. These resemble printed cotton bedspreads imported from India.

replaced ones of an earlier date. The paint is in poor condition, although patches of red, black, blue, brown and white are visible, with minute traces of gold leaf.

Scenes of agricultural labour including ploughing and fruit picking are illustrated, as are temples and houses. Village women are portrayed wearing *phasin* with red, black and white horizontal stripes, or *pha chong kaben* in similar patterns. The women are bare-breasted or wear a plain *pha sabai* over one shoulder or tied over the breasts. Their hair is arranged in a simple bun or worn loose. Men wearing *pha chong kaben* with a sheathed knife at the waist are ploughing and hoeing in the fields, and occasionally a glimpse of tattooed thigh is visible. In the scenes set inside houses and temples the costumes are more complex and ornate. Women wear *phasin* with patterns composed of red circles and swirls set on a black background. There is a resemblance between these faded patterns and the block prints made in India for the Siamese market. Attached to the printed, central panel is a wide red hem border. A *pha sabai* or a long-sleeved blouse is worn with the *phasin*. The women wear their hair in cone-shaped top knots framed with elaborate gold head-dresses, their necklaces are set with red stones (probably meant to represent rubies which were mined in Thailand and Burma), and they wear large golden discs as earrings. In one scene a group of soldiers appear in a doorway dressed in round-necked shirts and brimmed hats, brandishing long staves. In another scene dignitaries, carrying lotus-shaped fans, are portrayed in tall conical hats and floor-length, wide-sleeved robes with a cross-over neckline. Each set of mural paintings is enclosed within painted decorative borders of entwined flowers and leaves. Individual scenes are separated by clumps of coconut and palm trees, or groups of tile-roofed houses.

Wat Buak Khrok Luang

Wat Buak Khrok Luang is situated in a village on the outskirts of the city of Chiang Mai, north Thailand. The temple has carved wooden finials and eaves with a tiled roof and brick walls faced with stucco. The carvings and murals are attributed to the Tai Yai from the Shan states of Burma (Simatrang 1983). The Burmese were to influence the artists and craftsmen of Lanna, but the influence was not one way: in the Shan states they speak of some of their temples as being in the Chiang Mai style.

The Tai who settled in the river valleys in and around Chiang Mai are known as the Tai Yuan, and it is their local dress which predominates in the scenes of everyday life depicted in the murals of Wat Buak Khrok Luang. Women wear *phasin* with three distinct sections – sometimes the artist has drawn the stitch lines which join the three sections. The waistband is usually painted red, or red and

Temple mural painting, Wat Buak Khrok Luang, Chiang Mai province, depicting soldiers on horseback riding into battle, their tattoos visible beneath their *pha chong kaben*. Certain tattoo symbols were thought to bring courage and strength in battle.

white, and the central panel is in horizontal bands of colour of varying widths. The hem band is either red or red and black. Many village women are portrayed bare-breasted; others wear a *pha sabai* in plain blue or white, loosely folded over the shoulders. They wear their hair plaited in a bun, slightly to one side of the head, or in loops secured with a pin. In temple scenes some women wear gold bracelets. Village men wear *pha chong kaben* in plain colours or simple patterns, draped to just above the knee or drawn high on the hips to reveal thigh tattoos. In some scenes they wear *pha koma*, patterned like the *pha chong kaben*.

In court scenes the costumes are more elaborate and show a strong Burmese influence. Prince Siddhartha's wife is portrayed wearing a *phasin* with wavy bands in the central panel, representing Burmese *luntaya* patterns which are woven in a tapestry-weave technique and in Burma were reserved for royalty. The princess lies on a blanket with her head resting on triangular pillows with patterns of gold at each end. She wears gold chains in her hair, gold earrings, necklaces and bracelets. Her court attendants asleep nearby are dressed in Tai Yuan costume. Prince Siddhartha is portrayed in Lanna court costume, a gold head-dress shaped like a pagoda, a wide flat circle of gold around his neck, and gold bracelets. His long-sleeved jacket has winged epaulettes and is flaired below the waist with gold trimmings at the edge. A red and gold waist-sash completes the outfit. The prince wears a *pha chong kaben* with wavy bands, resembling the

148

Burmese *luntaya* pattern *lei sin kyo* (Aye Aye Mint 1980). All other important characters from the *jataka* stories (the previous lives of the Buddha) are also portrayed in Burmese costumes with *luntaya* patterns.

The court scenes include large floral-patterned textiles of black, red and blue which act as room-dividers and screens. Each screen consists of three squares of material with a central red circle surrounded by floral patterns contained within an outer square border. The block-print makers of Paithapur near Ahmedabad, northern India, were engaged in cutting blocks for printing Siam patterns. When shown photographs of the mural paintings they said that the patterns on the screens were like Indian woodblock-printed cotton, sold to be used as bedspreads and table-cloths.

During the eighteenth century the Lanna kingdom was subject to incursions from Burma, and Burmese and Siamese soldiers are portrayed in the murals. Siamese soldiers wear red, long-sleeved jackets with metal buttons and red helmets. Lanna and Burmese soldiers are portrayed riding horses and elephants into battle. They wear no special uniforms – their *pha chong kaben* are draped high over the hips to reveal leg tattoos of tigers and mythical animals, believed to bring courage and strength in battle. Weapons consist of wooden staves, knives and muskets. The horses' saddlery is decorated with golden tassels, and elephants have saddles, belts and head-coverings with gold and red trimmings.

The murals also contain scenes of Chinese labourers wearing loose-fitting blue jackets and square-legged trousers. In another scene a foreigner is depicted in trousers and jacket, holding what appear to be rosary beads.

Wat Phra Singh

Wat Phra Singh is the most venerated temple in the city of Chiang Mai. The temple was founded in 1345 by the seventh king of the Lanna kingdom, Phra Chao Payu, and the murals were painted in the early eighteenth century during the reign of King Thip Chang. Two walls are painted in the Lanna style and two in central Thai style. In the Lanna-style paintings the artist has portrayed life in the villages of the north with a special focus on costumes. The weaving patterns are painted using a fine brush so that it is possible to identify rows of plied yarns and the horizontal striped patterns which Tai Yuan women weave in their *phasin*. The hem bands are plain red or brown, except in a few scenes where there are examples of *teen jok*, black and red hem borders decorated with gold supplementary-weft patterns. Women are portrayed bare-breasted with *pha sabai* draped over the shoulders, or tied around the waist. The *pha sabai* have fine floral patterns with striped end-borders; many are monochrome – either red, blue, white, orange, green or

Far right Temple mural painting, Wat Phra Singh, Chiang Mai province, depicting two women dressed in central Thai style, with patterned *pha chong kaben*, probably printed cotton imported from India, and plain sashes. The cropped hair-style was also worn by men. One woman carries a paper umbrella, the other panniers. In the top right-hand corner is a man who also wears a printed *pha chong kaben*.

Temple mural painting, Wat Phra Singh, Chiang Mai province, depicting a Lanna lady framed in a gateway of the city wall. She wears a simple striped *phasin* with a sash draped over her shoulders. The man seated next to her wears a brief loincloth and white waist-sash. He is tattooed from waist to knee.

yellow. Women wear their hair pinned in a bun, often with a loose strand hanging at the back. Some are portrayed with long, straight hair without decoration. Working women wear no jewellery, but in scenes set in the palace of the governor of Chiang Mai they wear Tai Yuan *phasin* and gold earrings, and one woman is smoking a cheroot. The men wear plain *pha chong kaben* in red, yellow or blue fabric draped high on the hips to reveal thigh tattoos; some wear a belt or waist-sash. Over their shoulders they wear white *pha koma* with the ends hanging loose at the back. Some men wear flowers in their pierced earlobes; others use the hole to carry a cheroot.

Men and women from central Thailand are also portrayed in the murals. The women wear *pha chong kaben* to below the knee which are patterned with flowers, suggesting a printed cloth, possibly imported from India. They wear black or white *pha sabai* across the chest with part of the bosom exposed. Some women wear long chains of gold which extend to below the waist. Their hair-styles

are different from those of the women of Lanna, the hair shaved close to the head except for a circle on top which is trimmed like a brush. Men from central Thailand wear *pha chong kaben* with floral patterns, similar to those worn by the women, and shirts with mandarin collars in red, blue or green, some with a simple figured pattern or floral designs in white or gold. The shirts are buttoned at the front, some with a concealed fastening, and have long sleeves with cuffs. Shirts are tucked inside the *pha chong kaben* or are worn like jackets with a cut-away waist. A long sash knotted in front acts as a belt. The central Thai custom of men and women wearing similar costumes and hair-styles was fashionable in the nineteenth century.

In scenes portraying royalty the costumes are either Burmese or central Thai. Burmese princes and noblemen wear coiled lengths of white cloth resembling turbans, their top knots left uncovered. A small pony tail of hair is plaited through the coils of cloth, the end hanging loose. Some men wear only a single white headband. A Tai Yai prince wears a blue, long-sleeved shirt and over the top a fitted costume with winged epaulettes and a flared, scalloped border below the waistline. The pattern of his *pha chong kaben* resembles the *luntaya* pattern *maha kyo shwei taik*, meaning 'great line golden building' (Aye Aye Mint 1980). Over his shoulder he wears a sash woven in gold with red and green floral patterns. In one scene a group of Burmese court officials wear toga-like garments called *paso* (see pp. 32–3). The toga is formed from 10 yds (9 m) of fabric which is fastened around the waist, passes between the legs to form a kind of pantaloon, and then passes over the left shoulder and under the left arm. A round-necked shirt and long-sleeved jacket edged with gold are worn underneath. Tai Yai men have their thighs tattooed in a similar style to the Tai Yuan.

Central Thai court costumes are also portrayed in the murals. The head-dresses and fitted jackets are similar in shape to those worn by the princes of Lanna and Burma, but there is much more gold thread in the clothing and more gold jewellery is worn. Court-style *pha chong kaben* contain a high proportion of gold thread and may represent the gold brocaded silks which were imported from India at that time.

Palace interiors, both in the Lanna and central Thai-style murals, have curtains with floral patterns. Some are refined patterns probably printed or hand-painted in India, others have designs which suggest they are of European origin.

Wat Phumin and Wat Nong Bua

Wat Phumin and Wat Nong Bua are both situated in the Nan valley to the east of Chiang Mai. Wat Phumin was built in the sixteenth century by Chao Chetabut Phrohmin, ruler of Nan, which was a principality of the Lanna kingdom. The murals date from the mid-nineteenth century. Wat Nong Bua is situated in Ban Nong Bua, to the north of Nan. It is a small village temple and the murals are contemporary with those in Wat Phumin. The major Tai ethnic group living in the Nan valley are the Tai Lue, who migrated from Sipsong Panna, southern China, in the eighteenth and nineteenth centuries. There is some Keung script from Sipsong Panna printed over the murals. Costumes and textiles of royalty and villagers, the central Thai, Karens, Burmese and Europeans are portrayed.

Village women wear *phasin* similar in structure to those worn by the Tai Yuan of the Chiang Mai valley (see pp. 146–9). However, the central panel of the Tai Lue *phasin* has more complex weaving patterns. Plied yarns and multicoloured horizontal bands are interspersed with geometric and floral patterns drawn with a fine brush to resemble *matmi* or supplementary-weft patterns.

The *pha sabai* is little varied from the styles worn by the women of Chiang Mai, although a few are lined in red with a black and gold hem border. Some women wear long-sleeved blue jackets, either open at the front or tight-fitting with side-fastenings, which were a traditional part of Tai Lue costume worn in Sipsong Panna (Cheesman 1987). Women wear their hair in a bun on top of the head, decorated with flowers and ringed by chains of gold or silver. They wear thick cylinders of gold in their ears.

Tai Lue men are portrayed wearing *pha chong kaben* with small floral patterns, draped above the knee or mid-calf to reveal leg tattoos. They wear shoulder-sashes or round-necked shirts buttoned at the front with long sleeves. Their hair is shaved at the sides and trimmed short on top; some men wear sprigs of flowers and cylinders of metal or gold in their ears.

Tai Lue princesses wear *phasin* in the same patterns as village women, but the hem borders are decorated with gold. They wear flowing blue cloaks lined in red and exquisite gold chains set with rubies which pass around the body in swathes, ending in tassels set with tiny rubies. Gold chains encircle their hair, bracelets adorn their arms, and cylinders of gold decorate their ears. The most interesting portrait of a nobleman comes from Wat Phumin. He is thought to be Chao Ananta Wararitthidej, Governor of Nan from 1852 to 1891 (Simatrang 1983). He wears a mandarin-collared shirt under a front-buttoned jacket patterned with circles set in squares which are bordered by wavy patterns. This is probably of Chinese origin. A red cloak is draped over his shoulders, and he wears a plaid loincloth pleated at the front. His ears are decorated with sprigs of flowers, and his head is shaved except for a circle of hair on top.

Wat Phumin also contains a life-sized portrait of a young couple in Burmese court dress. She wears a *lungyi* with a Burmese *luntaya* pattern and a red blouse resembling a bustier. A black Burmese-style

jacket with tight sleeves completes the outfit. Cylinders of gold decorate her ears, and her hair is arranged in a top knot worn slightly to the left side. He wears his hair in a top knot kept in place with a white-knotted headband. His chest is tattooed in red circles and squares with dancing monkeys, thought to ward off evil spirits. His *lungyi* is decorated with the same pattern the lady wears, called a *puso* when worn by a man. Beneath the folds of the *lungyi* black tattoos of mythical animals are visible.

Wat Phumin also contains portraits of Europeans and Chinese. The style of trousers and jacket worn by a European man suggests the mid- to late nineteenth century (see p. 35). Hill-tribe men appear in one scene wearing scant loincloths with a few scattered tattoos on each thigh. They carry large bamboo baskets on their backs, and one smokes an opium pipe as he walks. Other scenes include Karen men in striped costumes.

In the murals of Wat Nong Bua there are screens made of blue and white cloth decorated with flowers resembling hibiscus. These do not have the repeat pattern format of an Indian block print and may be of Indonesian or Chinese origin.

Temple mural painting, Wat Phumin, Nan province, thought to be a portrait of Chao Ananta Wararitthidej, Governor of Nan, 1852–91. He wears a mandarin-collared shirt under a jacket, patterned with circles, squares and wavy patterns, probably of Chinese origin. He has a red cloak draped over his shoulders and a plaid loincloth, pleated at the front. His ears are decorated with sprigs of flowers and his head is shaved, except for a circle of hair on top trimmed like a brush.

8

✦

TEXTILES
OF NORTH-EAST
THAILAND

Detail of a cotton *phasin* from
Uttaradit province. The top panel
is woven in a supplementary-warp
pattern in black and green cotton.
The hem band is decorated
throughout with yellow cotton *jok*
patterns of diamonds, waves and
hooks bordered by yellow birds
and temple roofs with bird's-head
finials.

Extending eastwards from the
central plains of Thailand across the Korat plateau to the Mekong
river is the region of Thailand known as Isan. The people who live
in the area are mainly Tai Lao, although in the south, especially in
the provinces of Surin, Si Sa Ket and Buriram, there are villages
inhabited by Khmer, who settled in the region from Cambodia. Isan
consists of flat, undulating land with irregular rainfall and poor soil.
It has a history of poverty and deprivation. In the years when rainfall
is low large numbers of villagers migrate to the cities to find work,
leaving the elderly and mothers with young children in the villages.
In good years when rainfall is plentiful the people grow rice and
vegetables, cultivate mulberry for sericulture and, in some areas,
grow cotton.

North-east Thailand is famous for the quality of its silk and the
skill of the weavers. Silk was supplied to the regional courts of Nan
and Chiang Mai and also to Bangkok. Today this tradition continues:
silks brocaded with gold and silver thread and silks patterned with
matmi are commissioned from specialist weavers and worn by
wealthy women in Thailand and abroad.

The Lao, who settled in north-east Thailand, also moved west-
wards into the valleys bordering the central plains, in the provinces
of Uttaradit and Phichit. Here they interacted with Tai Lue and
Tai Yuan weavers, their costumes a blend of Lao weaving patterns
influenced by central and northern styles.

To the east of Uttaradit there are small mountain ranges and river
valleys, which were isolated until about twenty years ago when roads
were opened into the area. Two such areas are Nam Pat and Fah Tha
to the east of Uttaradit, where the weavers produce fine *phasin* in dis-

157

Left Detail of a silk and cotton *phasin*, Fah Tha, Uttaradit province. The top panel has bands of pink, purple, grey, ochre and green *matmi*, alternating with grey silk stripes. Between each pattern set are rows of brocaded white cotton in a geometric pattern. At the lower end is a wide band of brocaded cotton in zigzag and hook patterns.

Right Detail of a silk and cotton *phasin*, Nam Pat, Uttaradit province. The top panel of red, green, white and purple silk *matmi* in diamond patterns is echoed in the lower hem band of brocaded cotton.

tinctive patterns of silk *matmi* and intricate cotton brocade, interspersed with stripes. These *phasin* are admired for the richness and balance of the colours and the excellent quality of the weaving.

On the Korat plateau the weavers are famous for the silk *matmi* they produce in a great variety of patterns and colours. Derived from nature and including stylised flowers, trees, fruit, animals and birds, these complex patterns are interspersed with squares, triangles, circles, zigzags and stripes. They require skill at the tying and dyeing stages and when the patterned yarn is woven (see Chapter 3). *Matmi* patterns are given descriptive names by the weavers, mostly flowers, plants, trees and animals. Some are named after the village or district where they are woven. The following list of patterns was collected in the villages of north-east Thailand.

cobra	diamonds	dragon
king of snakes	waves	bamboo
trees	water melon	lions
birds	turtle	butterflies
serpent	cones	elephants
weeds	stripes	rice
white flower	hooks	water hyacinth
rocket	squid	
melon seed	spider	

Women wear *matmi* in the centre panels of their *phasin* skirts. The *phasin* has three sections: a waistband with a supplementary-weft

159

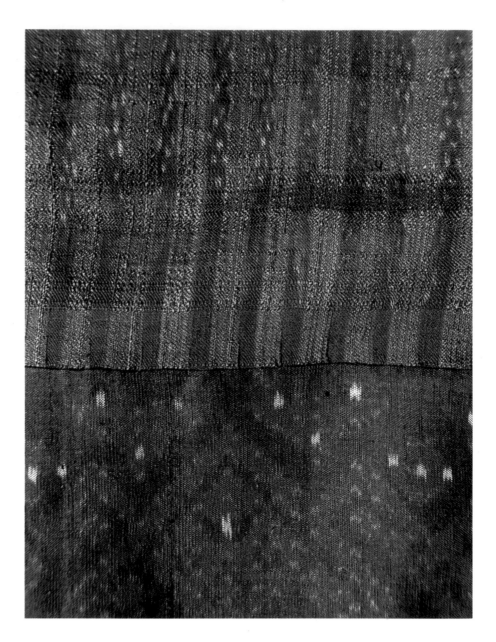

Detail of a silk *phasin* from Surin province. The main panel is woven in a *matmi* pattern called bamboo leaf. The hem border has diamond *matmi* patterns. The rich colours are characteristic of this region of Thailand.

pattern, often woven of silk; a central panel of *matmi*; and a hem band with a supplementary-weft pattern. The waistband often has a vertical striped pattern, and the hem border is narrow, usually 3–4 in (7.6–10 cm) wide, and woven in cotton, often in lengths of several yards or metres and cut as required. Women either weave the borders at home or buy them in a local store or market-place.

The Isan *phasin* reflects the age and social status of the wearer. Young women wear vibrant designs and in middle age they wear more subdued colours and patterns, often known as '*phasin* for grandmothers'. In old age dark, rich hues are worn. In recent years weavers have begun to create *phasin* in two sections instead of three. They tie simple *matmi* patterns in the top section of the warp, to serve as the waistband, and complex patterns in the rest of the

160

A Phu Tai lady wearing a red silk *pha prae wa* (also illustrated on cover and p. 6) with supplementary-weft patterns in blue, green, white and orange silk. The Phu Tai are famous for their finely patterned silk textiles.

warp. A separate hem border is then added. From old photographs and mural paintings it is evident that the traditional Isan *phasin* was worn above the ankle or to mid-calf.

The Isan provinces of Surin, Si Sa Ket and Buriram lie to the south of Isan, bordering Cambodia. The Khmer, who have settled in the three provinces, weave textiles with Khmer *matmi* patterns which require great skill in the tying of the weft. The colours are rich, muted shades of red, purple and green with flashes of yellow and black. The *phasin* are woven in three sections – a striped waistband with a supplementary weft and *matmi* patterns in the central panel and hem band.

With their *phasin* women wear shoulder-sashes, called *pha biang*. For everyday wear these were plain cotton, but to attend temple

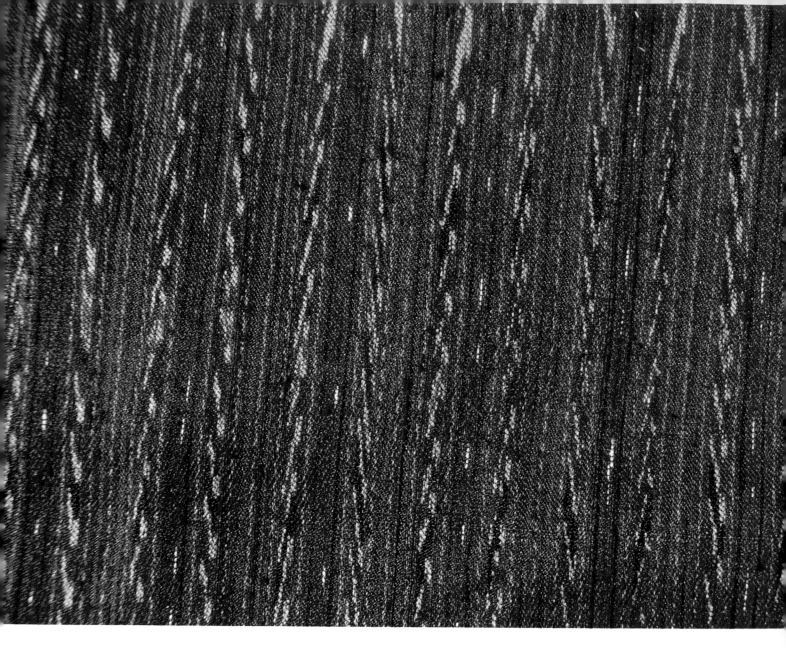

Detail of a *matmi pha chong kaben*,
Surin province.

ceremonies the women wear white silk. The Phu Tai from the provinces of Kalasin, Mukdahan and Ubon weave red silk sashes
called *pha prae wa*. These are extremely colourful with complex
supplementary-weft patterns and are worn wrapped over the
breasts as a type of sleeveless camisole.

The Khmer weave silk *pha chong kaben* which are worn by both
men and women. These contain fine, rich *matmi* patterns in the
central field with a narrow decorative panel at the selvage. For court
wear the *pha chong kaben* were woven with complex central panels
of *matmi* and elaborate end-borders.

Evidence from nineteenth-century mural paintings in north-east
Thailand suggests that patterned *pha chong kaben* were also worn by
the Tai Lao. The patterns portrayed are simple stripes and checks.
Today the *pha chong kaben* has been replaced in many areas by indigo
trousers or a plaid sarong. The sarong is a rectangular length of
fabric sewn to form a tube which is tucked with a pleat at the waist.
The patterns can be complex – bands of plain and plied yarns in
varying shades and colours arranged in the warp, the sequence then

162

Detail of a *pha chong kaben*, Surin province, woven in the *matmi* pattern called bamboo leaf.

Pages 164–5 Detail of a silk *pha koma*, Khon Kaen province. The warp has bands of black, white, green and red silk with corresponding bands in the weft to create a plaid. The end-borders have a wide red stripe.

repeated in the weft. Alternatively the weft may be arranged in a different sequence creating a shot and plied plaid which appears to shimmer in the light (see p. 108). The brightest colours are worn by young men; the elderly wear more sombre plaids.

In the villages men are rarely without a length of plaid cloth, called a *pha koma*, which serves as a turban, a waist-sash, a bathing wrap, or simply to mop sweat from the body. Strung between bamboo poles on a stand, it may serve as a baby's cradle. For these ordinary purposes the *pha koma* is woven in cotton. On ceremonial occasions it is worn as a shoulder-sash, and the weavers produce fine silk plaids with decorative borders which sometimes include gold and silver thread.

Wat Chai Sri

Wat Chai Sri is situated in Ban Sawathi, Khon Kaen province. The temple is built of brick and stucco, surrounded by a low wall decorated with wooden horses. The murals which are seen on interior and exterior walls are dated by Thai scholars to the mid- to late

163

Far right Temple mural painting, with decorated border, on the exterior wall of Wat Sra Bua Kaew, Khon Kaen province, illustrating the costumes and textile patterns of Isan.

A villager from Ban Na Ka, Udon Thani province, wearing a long-sleeved indigo cotton blouse and cotton indigo *matmi phasin*. Her palm-leaf hat is typical of those worn for working in the fields.

nineteenth century (Samosorn 1989). Painted in blue, black, yellow and yellow ochre, the colours were obtained from indigo, turmeric and earth pigments, and the black used for outlines made locally either from soot or imported ink from China. The limited palette used by the artist does not reflect the range of coloured yarns woven by Tai Lao weavers, although indigo-dyed cotton is common wear for villagers when working in the fields. The murals portray women wearing *phasin* and blouses ranging from pale blue to blue-black, illustrating the range of shades available to the indigo dyer, depending on the number of times the cloth was immersed in the dye bath (see Chapter 3). Many *phasin* have patterns with stripes and dots representing indigo cotton *matmi*. With the *phasin* women wear round-necked, long-sleeved, indigo blouses, fastened at the side with rows of tiny buttons. Over the blouses they wear white *pha biang* as sashes. For jewellery they wear gold hair-clips and gold bracelets over the blouse sleeves. Some carry black parasols as protection from the sun. Men are portrayed wearing blue *pha chong kaben* to below the knee or a little above to reveal leg tattoos. They are bare-chested or wear blue, round-necked, front-buttoned shirts and narrow-brimmed hats resembling the woven palm-leaf hats worn by many farmers today.

Wat Sra Bua Kaew

The temple of Wat Sra Bua Kaew, Nong Song Hong, Khon Kaen province is constructed of brick faced with stucco. The murals, which are dated to the early twentieth century, are painted in indigo, yellow ochre, brown, black, turquoise and green. The women's *phasin* have narrow waistbands, often plain white or with black and white geometric patterns. The central panels are portrayed in a variety of geometric and linear patterns which resemble *matmi* and supplementary-weft patterns, called *khit* in north-east Thailand. The hem borders are narrow bands also resembling supplementary-weft patterns.

Pha biang in plain colours or with small floral patterns are worn across one shoulder and over the breasts. Some women wear sleeveless, round-necked blouses with a *pha biang* as a sash on top. They wear their hair cut short above the ears and decorated with metal clips. Tai Lao men wear *pha chong kaben* of blue or turquoise cloth sometimes decorated with fine geometric lines. The garment is worn to mid-calf length or above the knee to reveal leg tattoos. Some men are bare-chested; others wear short-sleeved, round-necked shirts with patterned *pha koma* over the top. Their hats are narrow-brimmed and made of palm leaf like those portrayed in Wat Chai Sri. Both men and women carry parasols to protect them from the sun.

9

❖

TEXTILES OF CENTRAL AND SOUTH THAILAND

Detail of a *phasin* from Sukhothai. The hem border is decorated with *jok* patterns of diamonds and triangles in red, white, black and yellow cotton.

The central plains are the fertile heartland of Thailand, a seemingly endless patchwork of rice fields, the traditional source of wealth. For 700 years a dependable water-supply has been maintained through complex systems fed by several major rivers. The Tai settled here from the mountain valleys to establish great Buddhist cities, and a network of villages and small towns along the rivers and canals (*klongs*). The southern peninsula is a contrasting world, being mainly a Muslim society, its people sustained by rich, coastal fishing waters, rubber plantations and tin-mines. The textiles of the central plains and the south fall into three loose categories: the textiles of the Tai, showing some similarities with the weaving patterns of the north and north-east; textiles from the southern peninsula, influenced by Malay patterns; and thirdly, imported textiles, many commissioned by the court and senior officials in the cities.

In the eighteenth century, during the reign of Rama I, large numbers of Tai Phuan, also called Lao Phuan, who migrated from Xieng Khouang province, Laos (Cheesman 1988), were settled on the central plains, many in villages around Uttaradit and Sukhothai. They weave *phasin* in bold, vibrant colours, constructed of four woven bands sewn together with a decorative stitch. The waistband is made of two strips of plain-weave cotton sewn together at the selvage, the central panel is woven in a supplementary-warp pattern, and the hem border has a wide band of *jok*.

South of Uttaradit and south-east of Sukhothai lies the province of Phichit, with its capital situated in the Nan river valley. The province is bordered by the central plains to the west and the Korat plateau of Isan to the east. Tai Lao immigrants were forcibly settled

169

Detail of a silk and cotton *phasin*, Phichit province. The main panel is woven in a complex *matmi* pattern of hooks, diamonds and flowers in red, purple, blue and green silk. The hem border has a red cotton ground weave with a brocaded geometric pattern in yellow, red, green, black and white cotton.

in the area at the beginning of the nineteenth century. The *phasin* of Phichit are distinguished by the predominance of red in the patterns. Red dye is obtained from *krang*, and the people are known as Lao Krang because of the red dye which dominates their costumes. They weave *matmi* patterns in the main panel of the *phasin*, which often has no separate waistband. Unlike the horizontal patterns of Chiang Mai and Nan, the patterns run vertically from waist to hem border. The hem borders are brocaded in brightly coloured cotton or silk, with a band of plain weave at the bottom.

Southern peninsula Thailand was once part of the Buddhist Śrivijayan kingdom (seventh to twelfth centuries) of the Indonesian archipelago. At later times in history the area came under the influence of the Malay states, the border between the two countries being constantly redefined. The southern states were administered from the provincial capital of Nakhon Si Thammarat, its rulers owing allegiance to the king in Bangkok. During the skirmishes between the southern Thai and Malay states local people were often displaced. In 1811 following an uprising in Kedah the ruler of Nakhon Si Thammarat took a number of prisoners, including Muslim weavers, to settle in the vicinity of Nakhon Si Thammarat. The weavers were skilled at creating *songket*, Malay patterns using multi-coloured silks and gold and silver thread. Local women were trained in this technique, and Nakhon Si Thammarat became famous for the delicate, gold-patterned textiles woven for the exclusive use of local rulers (Fraser-Lu 1988). It is possible that descendants of the Muslim weavers settled in Bangkok, continuing with their traditional skills, which in the 1950s were important in the setting up of Jim Thompson's silk business (see p. 103).

The Thai living in the cities of the central plains, the Chao Phya river basin and in southern peninsula Thailand have a long history of contact with foreign governments and traders. The Chinese settled along the trade routes throughout South-East Asia and became middle men, dealing in a wide variety of goods, from herbs and spices, metals and ceramics to damasks, velvets, satins, silk and gold thread (Hall 1964). Arab and Indian merchants were also important in the history of the textile trade. By the fifteenth century they had converted much of the Malay peninsula and southern Thailand to Islam. Muslim traders brought Indian textiles from Gujarat and the Coromandel coast to ports throughout South-East Asia.

In the seventeenth century the trade was taken over by European companies. When Ayuthya was capital (1350–1767), the city was connected by river and an extensive network of waterways south to the sea ports. The kings of Ayuthya monopolised foreign trade and gained vast revenues which supported the luxurious life-style of the court. This was the age of European kings who ruled by the doctrine of divine right. A similar Khmer concept of a god king was upheld at the court of Ayuthya, where lavish textiles and jewellery gave visual credence to this belief. At provincial courts like Nan and Chiang Mai, where Buddhist doctrine prevailed, court costumes were more restrained. In the city of Ayuthya craftsmen set up workshops in specialist neighbourhoods, serving the city and the court. Elaborate gold jewellery and ornaments survive from this period, but lack of material evidence leads us only to assume that local weavers were supplying equally rich textiles to the court.

Evidence of imported fabrics are easier to trace through the documents of the Indian and European trading companies, who from the fifteenth century were supplying textiles and yarn from India, China, the Middle East and Europe. Gold brocades, *patola* (double-

Page 174 Textile, made in India for the Thai market, 18th-century. The central field has a maroon-black background with stamp-resist leaf patterns entwined around the torso images of *thepanum* which have been freely drawn and dye-resisted, then stamped with gold.

Page 175 Temple ceiling decoration of gold stencilled patterns, Wat Suwannaram, Thonburi, near Bangkok. These designs are similar to printed textile patterns produced in India for the Thai market.

Right Printed cotton textile imported from India for the general market, *c.* 19th century.

Left Fragment of an 18th-century painted and dye-resist printed cotton in red, blue-green and tan vegetable dyes, made in India for the Thai market. The blue, red and tan geometric designs in the central field have been freely drawn, and each set contains a dye-resist pattern of flowers and leaves. The border, with a blue-painted background, contains dancing figures which have been drawn and dye-resisted. The figures are interspersed with leaf patterns which are painted and contain small dye-resist flower patterns. (For preservation purposes the fragments have been mounted on a red silk background.)

ikat) silks, resist-patterned cottons, linens, velvet and lace were all popular (Chumbala 1985). But the court at Ayuthya did not accept foreign designs on printed fabrics, preferring to send patterns for copying by overseas craftsmen. During the reign of King Narai (1656–88) court designers were dispatching pattern books to India to be copied and printed in specified colours.

In India evidence of this trade in printed textiles can be found in the block-makers' workshops of Gujarat, where collections of pattern books containing Thai designs, with instructions written in central Thai, have been kept. The designs are known to the block-makers as 'Siam patterns'. These pattern books were sent from Ayuthya or Bangkok to agents in Surat who commissioned the blocks. Once cut the patterned blocks were sent directly to printers' workshops in Ahmedabad. The pattern books contain floral, animal and geometric designs and pendant patterns used as end-borders. These designs were printed on cotton with dye or dye resist. Other pat-

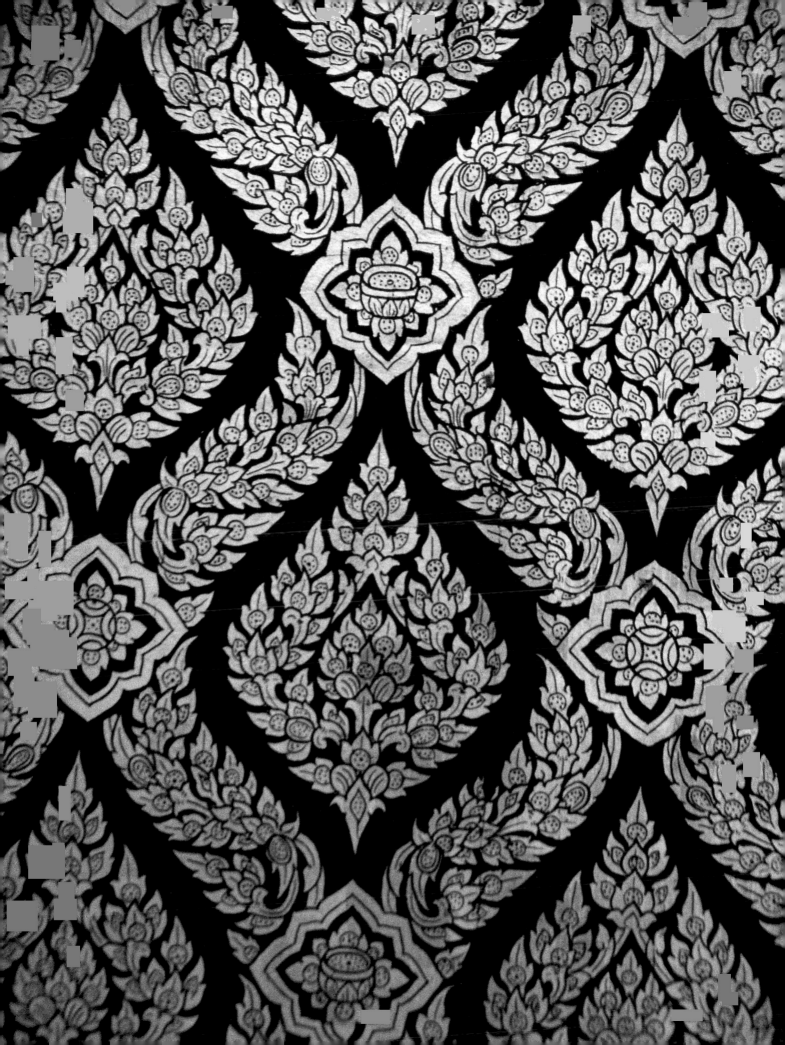

terns, such as *thepanum* (angels) and human figures, were freely drawn. In this area of the designs it is not always possible to be sure of the origin of the patterns. Although the *thepanum* are Thai in origin, some of the human figures may represent characters from Indian mythology. Indian workshops produced printed cotton lengths for *pha chong kaben*, with a central field and end-borders, worn by both men and women. Cotton was also printed in lengths of 10 yds (9 m), narrower than a sari, and lengths without borders which may have been used as curtains and room-dividers (verbal communication with Maneklal T. Gajjar, 1990).

According to the owner of one workshop, 'Siam patterns' were still being cut in the time of his grandfather, although it is probable that his forebears and other families of master block-makers in Gujarat have been involved in the trade for centuries. It was the tradition that the agents from Surat came once a year to settle accounts and make gifts to the block-makers. Special ceremonies were held when businesses passed from one generation to the next. The impression is of an old-established trade going back many generations. Block-printed textiles were imported to Ayuthya in large quantities. In 1690 the king decided to stem the flow by producing the cloth locally. With the aid of the Dutch he acquired cotton seeds and dyes from India and employed Indian craftsmen to train locals in printing and dyeing techniques. There are no records of the results of this venture (Gittinger 1982).

By the late eighteenth century, when the capital moved to Bangkok, Indian traders were flooding the market with cruder, block-printed versions of the earlier fine designs. These simpler patterns appear more Indian than Thai and continued to be popular in the nineteenth century. In 1855 Sir John Bowring, Minister Plenipotentiary to China, visited Bangkok and commented on the taste for Indian fabrics.

> At the present time, persons fancy *pa nungs* [*pha chong kaben*]. Chintz pleases the men. *Pa nungs* of alternate stripes of silk and gold thread, also chintz of a small blue and white check, with gold thread borders pleases the women. A *pa nung* is about three yards of strong Indian chintz, of star pattern on deep red, blue, green and chocolate coloured grounds. The Siamese place the middle of this, when opened, to the small of the back, bringing the two ends round the body before and the upper edges being twisted together are tucked in between the body and the cloth. The part hanging is folded in large pleats, passed between the legs and tucked in behind as before.

When the capital moved from Ayuthya to Bangkok, craftsmen again set up shops in specialist neighbourhoods. Weavers and dyers lived in wooden houses along the waterways (*klongs*) where they could

A silk *pha chong kaben* of Indian or Thai origin worn by the consort of Rama V (1868–1910). The end-borders are woven in lilac and purple silk, brocaded with gold thread.

wash and process yarn. In the time of King Rama IV (1851–68) it was the custom for many wealthy families to maintain craftsmen in their own houses. Goldsmiths, silversmiths, weavers and lacquer workers were among those employed in this way. At the beginning of the twentieth century there were still many workshops producing beautiful brocades and fine silks for the court. One example was Sermsiri which provided much of the fabric used for the 1925 coronation of Rama VII (Chumbala 1985). Skilled weavers in the provinces also provided *matmi* and brocaded silks for the court. Princess Boonchiradorn Chutatuij (1897–1979), who came to Bangkok from north-east Thailand, regularly ordered silks woven in the patterns of Ubon (see p. 178). When her mother, Mom Boonyern, joined her in 1922, she brought weavers from Ubon to set up a small workshop at court (Chumbala 1985). In 1947 Dr M. Smith, physician to the court, commented on the skill of provincial weavers.

In the two chief towns in the north, namely Chiang Mai and Korat where the industry had been in existence for hundreds of years,

A collection of silks woven in north and north-east Thailand, worn at court by Princess Boonchiradorn Chutatuij (1897–1979).

weaving had attained a very high degree of perfection. For intricacy of design and richness of colouring the fabrics made there compared well with any of their kind made in other countries. They provided the materials for the dress and robes of office worn by nobles and officials at court functions.

Although indigenous textiles survived competition from imports, they were constantly threatened. In the nineteenth century there was alarm at the large quantities of raw silk being imported from China. The government responded with a sericulture programme to try and increase local production. In 1903 40,000 to 60,000 people on the Korat plateau were engaged in sericulture, and there were twenty-three merchants dealing in silk yarn (Brown 1980). But the greatest threat to traditional textiles came when Western fashions

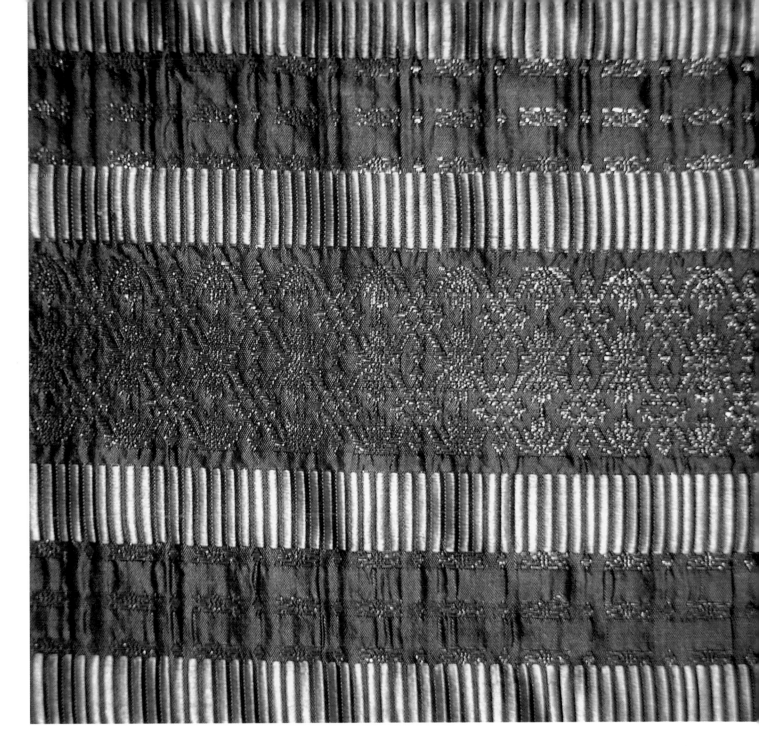

Detail of the hem border of a *phasin*, Bangkok, 20th century. Black silk warp and gold silk weft, brocaded with gold thread.

were imposed in the 1930s and 40s. The weaving of silk brocades and other special patterns dwindled in the workshops of Bangkok, as Jim Thompson was to discover when he set up his silk enterprise in the 1950s. Fortunately he found some families of Muslim weavers settled along the *klongs* who were able to meet his requirements (Warren 1970).

Weaving specialist textiles for the court in Bangkok is a tradition which survived the period of Westernisation. In north-east Thailand Pa Payom of Roi Et wove blue and white silk for royal procession robes and for the king yellow silk with gold-brocaded patterns which include *thepanum* (verbal communication, 1983). Today master weavers continue to produce superb *matmi*, many pieces as fine as those fashionable decades ago at court.

Temple mural painting, Bangkok, late 18th-century. The figures portray the classical mask-like expressions and gracious gestures of royalty and ascetics. The costumes are arranged to complement the elegant postures.

Today the Thai silk industry exports silk for clothing and upholstery to all the major industrial countries. With the help of government and charitable institutions weaving is promoted throughout the rural areas. The market for traditional Thai textiles has been supported by Her Majesty Queen Sirikit (see p. 103), so that a balance is kept between the demands of Western markets and

the need to keep alive the weaving of textiles which are uniquely Thai in character.

The mural paintings of central Thailand conform to stricter rules of representation than those painted by the artists of north and north-east Thailand. The human figure is depicted according to his or her spiritual nature, or rank in society. Bodhisattvas, ascetics and royalty wear mask-like expressions and have gracious gestures and postures. Their faces are shown in profile or three-quarter view, with arched eyebrow, elongated eye and eyelid and a slightly smiling mouth. The body is graceful and proportioned in a set artistic vocabulary, which makes the characters appear more as shadow puppets than humans (Wray, Rosenfield and Bailey 1972). However, commoners are portrayed as real human beings, with physical characteristics that are not necessarily flattering, such as coarse features and stocky builds. There is also a code for the portrayal of landscape. Royalty are set apart in gold-leaf palaces, dressed in elaborate costumes with crowns and tiered umbrellas of gold, signifying their rank. Their costumes are arranged to complement their elegant postures, flat patterns of gold leaf with precise folds which balance the overall composition of the scene. Court interiors are richly decorated with geometric and floral patterns, in a flat, two-dimensional style resembling the miniature court paintings of the Moguls. The physical landscape, trees, rivers and plants are often painted in a more expressive and realistic style, like that used for ordinary people.

Wat Suwannaram, Thonburi

Wat Suwannaram was founded in the seventeenth century, restored in the eighteenth century and again in the reign of Rama III (1824–51). The temple is situated in Thonburi, the capital of Siam between 1767 and 1782, before the founding of Bangkok. The *wat* buildings are constructed of brick and stucco, with orange-tiled roofs and wooden finials shaped like birds. The murals were painted by two artists in the classic central Thai style. Royalty are portrayed wearing *pha chong kaben* of gold brocade with green, red or black floral patterns. Prince Vessantura wears a gold brocade jacket with winged epaulettes and floral patterns at the neck and cuffs. The women wear elaborate collars of gold with their arms and wrists decorated with gold chains and medallions. They wear conical, gold head-dresses with winged side panels covering the ears. The jewellery is similar in pattern to the bracelets and head-dresses excavated at Ayuthya (National Museum). Royal attendants wear patterned *pha chong kaben* with front-buttoned jackets lined in red and waist-sashes with gold end-borders. Their hair is shaved close to the head, except for a circle on top trimmed like a brush. Female attendants wear patterned *pha chong kaben* and pleated shoulder-sashes.

181

10

❖

CONCLUSION

Silk weft *matmi phasin*, Roi Et province, north-east Thailand.

The arts of South-East Asia are often viewed as an extension of Indian and Chinese culture, and not enough emphasis is placed on the indigenous creativity of the region. Unlike many of its neighbours Thailand avoided colonisation, and its treasures did not accumulate in Western museums to be studied and catalogued by foreign scholars. The country suffered repeated pillage and destruction of its heritage over many centuries as a result of wars with Burma. The material culture of cities like Sukhothai were virtually destroyed, leaving remains of brick and stone monuments to be reconstructed by later communities. Nevertheless, the cultural institutions and universities of Thailand are continuously documenting new sites of historic importance. In the last ten years Thai scholars have rediscovered isolated temples in the north-east with fascinating mural paintings portraying life in that part of rural Thailand. Some have been chosen to illustrate costume and textile patterns in this book. Although evidence of the artistic and cultural traditions of the Thai can be seen in many temples, museums and institutions throughout the country, sadly there is no comprehensive textile museum where the ancient arts of women, who are the traditional weavers and dyers, are given adequate recognition.

In village society textiles are the most important expression of the creativity of women. The loom acts as a symbol of womanhood, its special significance acknowledged by men who will not touch a loom once it is set up and in use. Women gain spiritual merit from weaving ceremonial textiles for the monastery and robes for the monks. A skilled weaver is a respected member of the village and has some status within the monastic community. In north-east Thailand abbots

183

and senior monks are familiar with the skill levels of weavers in the local villages and have a say in the iconography used in the weaving patterns. The association between village men and the monasteries has been widely documented, but the role of women has often been considered only within the context of domestic duties. Clearly their role is more creative and culturally valuable.

There are two major textile traditions in Thailand – village and court – although they are interrelated as in other South-East Asian societies. In the courts of central Thailand, at Sukhothai and Ayuthya and later Bangkok there was a tradition of importing lavish brocaded and printed textiles from India and silks from China. These were necessary to support the dignity of the court which upheld the Khmer concept of a god king, his subjects dressed in a level of grandeur defined by rank. The court was particular about the kind of fabrics imported. Designs were often strictly controlled, the Thais sending pattern books and instructions to the producers abroad. However, at the regional courts most costumes were woven locally in the traditional patterns of the area, rank being indicated by the amount of gold and silver thread used in the weaving of indigenous patterns. Thailand's élite group of highly skilled weavers continue the tradition of creating *matmi* silks and brocades for members of the royal family, discerning Thais and overseas buyers.

Traditional designs have also been adapted to meet the demands of Western markets. Clothing, upholstery fabrics, curtains, table-linen and gift items are marketed through commercial companies, or through charitable organisations which often support weavers in the rural areas. Thai silk and cotton are sold by the yard or metre in an astounding array of rich and subtle colours. The choice is enormous. The Thais have achieved a good reputation for the quality and style of their hand-woven textiles. They are modern and innovative and can compete in the international luxury-goods market.

Thai silk has a slub and sheen and resistance to creasing which make it a very desirable fabric. It owes these unique qualities to indigenous silk cocoons which produce a slubby thread and the hand-reeling process which enhances the sheen. Currently in the commercial sector imported silk dupion is used for the warp and Thai silk yarn for the weft. As the demand for weft increases there is pressure to improve the level of local production. One way of achieving this is by replacing native cocoons with foreign hybrids to produce a cash-crop. As traditional sericulture is carried out in harmony with the rice cycle, this may threaten the integrated nature of village production.

The introduction of hybrid cocoons in the villages of Thailand does not automatically ensure a higher yield. Imported silk cocoons must adapt to the hot and humid climate and are susceptible to local pests and diseases. Higher standards of hygiene and protection are necessary but not always achievable in the villages, except in wealthy households. From a market standpoint it is important to retain the unique character of Thai silk. If the warp is imported and the weft produced from foreign hybrids, then sericulturalists must keep a balance between production and the character of the yarn. It would be a sad loss if Thai silk became indistinguishable from silk produced in other parts of Asia.

As textile production becomes more standardised and mechanised throughout the world the unique quality of indigenous, hand-spun, hand-woven cloth becomes appreciated as a rare and valued commodity. What is not so easily understood is the importance of hand-woven textiles in traditional village society, a theme explored in Chapter 2. However, times are changing. In the last few years packets of machine-manufactured, plastic-wrapped robes and blankets are replacing hand-woven textiles presented as gifts to the monks. Many girls no longer learn the techniques for weaving banners and other ceremonial items. In north-east Thailand more women every year migrate from poor villages to the cities to find work, leading to a breakdown in family relationships. The days of the rice cycle and integrated weaving culture may be numbered.

However, the Thais are an artistic people and quick to adapt to changing conditions. There are dedicated women in Thailand who devote their time to promoting and preserving the unique character of Thai textiles and giving support to the weavers. Her Majesty Queen Sirikit (see pp. 103, 180) has provided important leadership in this field. It is hoped that this book will promote an interest in Thai textiles not only in a historical and cultural context but as examples of a living craft. If textile production is in transition, then this book serves as a reminder that in Thailand textiles are not merely a commodity but a symbol of the well-balanced rhythms of social and religious custom.

Manuscript painting of a lady in traditional northern Thai costume, Wat Nong Bua, Nan province.

BIBLIOGRAPHY

ANON, 1895 (repr. n.d.). *Report of a Survey in Siam: An Englishman's Siamese Journals 1890–1893*, Siam Media International, Bangkok

ARCHAMBAULT, M. 1989. 'Blockprinted fabrics of Gujarat for export to Siam: An encounter with Mr Maneklal T. Gajjar', *Journal of the Siam Society*, Vol. 77, Pt 2

AYE AYE MINT (ed.) 1980. *Burmese Acheik Patterns from an old Parabaik Manuscript*, Rangoon

BOCK, C. 1884 (repr. 1986). *Temples and Elephants: Travels in Siam 1881–1882*, Oxford University Press, Singapore

BOISSELIER, J. 1976. *Thai Painting*, Kodansha International, Tokyo

BOWRING, SIR J. (repr. 1969). *The Kingdom and People of Siam*, Oxford University Press, Kuala Lumpur

BROWN, I. 1980. 'Government, Initiative and Peasant response in the Siamese silk industry', *Journal of the Siam Society*, Vol. 68, Pt 2

CHEESMAN, P., and SONGSAK, P. 1987. *Lan Na Textiles, Yuan Lue Lao*, Center for the Promotion of Arts and Culture, Chiang Mai University, Thailand

CHEESMAN, P. 1988. *Lao Textiles: Ancient Symbols, Living Art*, White Lotus Co. Ltd, Bangkok

CHONGKOL, C. 1982. 'Textiles and costume in Thailand', *Arts of Asia*, Nov.

CHONGKOL, C., and WOODWARD, H. jun. 1966. *Guide to the U Thong National Museum, Suphanburi*, Fine Arts Department, Bangkok

CHUMBALA, M.L. 1985. 'The Textile Collection of Princess Boonchiradorn', B.A. thesis, Winchester School of Art, U.K.

COEDES, G. 1966. *The Making of South East Asia*, Routledge & Kegan Paul Ltd, London

COMMITTEE FOR THE PROMOTION OF THAI SILK PRODUCTS, MINISTRY OF INDUSTRY, THAILAND. 1983. *Matmi (Ikat textiles)*, Prachachon Co. Ltd, Bangkok

CRAIB, W.G. 1926. *Florae Siamensis*, Siam Society, Bangkok

CURTIS, L.J. 1903. *The Laos of North Siam*, Westminster Press, Philadelphia

DEPARTMENT OF INDUSTRIAL PROMOTION, MINISTRY OF INDUSTRY, 1986. *Khit: Supplementary Weft Textiles*, Brainbox Publishers, Bangkok

DISKUL, M.C. SUBHADRADIS. 1970. *Art in Thailand: A Brief History*, Krung Siam Press, Bangkok

DIVISION OF EDUCATION, 1964. *The Revised Ancient Documents: Book 4*, Bangkok

DUNCAN, H. 1971. *Techniques of Traditional Thai Painting*, Sawaddi Special Edition, pp. 56–8

FRASER-LU, SYLVIA. 1988. *Handwoven Textiles of South-East Asia*, Oxford University Press, Singapore

GILMAN D'ARCY, P. (trans.) 1967. *Notes on the customs of Cambodia by Chou Ta Kuan 1300–1312 A.D.* (trans. from French version by Paul Pelliot), Social Science Association, Bangkok

GITTINGER, M. 1979. *Splendid Symbols: Textiles and Tradition in Indonesia*, Textile Museum, Washington, DC

GITTINGER, M. (ed.) 1980. *Indonesian Textiles, Irene Emery Roundtable on Museum Textiles, 1979 Proceedings*, Textile Museum, Washington, DC

GITTINGER, M. 1982. *Master Dyers to the World*, Textile Museum, Washington, DC

GRISWOLD, A.B., and PRASERT NA NAGARA. 1967. 'Epigraphic and Historical Studies No. 9: the inscription of Ramkamhaeng of Sukhothai (1292 A.D.)', *Journal of the Siam Society* LX, 2, Bangkok, pp. 179–228

GROSLIER, G. 1921. *Recherches sur les Cambodgiens*, Paris

HADDON, A.C., and START, L.E. (repr. 1982). *Iban or Sea Dyak Fabrics and Their Patterns: A Descriptive Catalogue*, Ruth Bean, Carlton, Bedford

HALL, D.G.E. 1964. *A History of South East Asia*, Macmillan, London

HALLET, HOLT S. (repr. 1889). 'My first visit to Zimme', *Blackwood's magazine*, William Blackwood & Son Ltd, Edinburgh

HENRIKSON, M.A. 1978. *A Preliminary Note on Some Northern Thai Woven Patterns*, Lampang Reports, Publication no. 5. (ed. S. Egerod and P. Sorenson), Scandinavian Institute of Asian Studies, special publications, Bangkok

HOWES, M. 1974. 'Thai Silk at the Crossroads', *Investor Magazine*, Oct., pp. 611–16

HUDSON, R. 1965. *Hudson's Guide to Chiang Mai and the North*, Thai Celadon Co., Bangkok

INNES, R.A. 1957. *Costumes of Upper Burma and the Shan States in the Collections of Bankfield Museum*, Halifax Museums, Halifax

IRWIN, J., and SCHWARTZ, P. 1966. *Indo-European Textile History*, Calico Museum of Textiles, Ahmedabad

JAYAWICKRAMA, N.A. 1962. *The Sheaf of Garlands of The Epochs of the Conqueror (1528 A.D.)*, (trans. of 'Jinakalamalipakaranam of Ratanapanna Thera'), Ceylon

JUMSAI, M. 1967. *History of Laos*, Chalermit, Bangkok

KEYES, C. 1965. 'Isarn in a Thai state, a brief survey of the Thai "Northeastern Problem"', *Seminar on Asia Studies*, 502, Thailand

KEYES, C.F. 1967. *Isarn Regionalism in North east Thailand*, Interim report no. 10, S.E. Asia Program data paper no. 65, Cornell Thailand Project, Cornell University, Ithaca

KLAUSNER, W. 1981. *Reflections on Thai Culture*, published privately, Bangkok

KRUG, S. and DUBOFF, S. 1982. *The Kamthieng House*, The Siam Society, Bangkok

KUNSTADTER, P. (ed.) 1967. *South-east Asian Tribes, Minorities and Nations*, Vol. 1, Princeton University Press, Princeton

LAUNAY, A. 1920. *Histoire de la Mission du Siam*, Documents Historiques, Vol. 1, Paris

LEADBEATER, E. 1979. *Spinning and Spinning Wheels*, Shire Album 43, Shire Publications, Herts

LEFFERTS, L. 1978. 'Northeast Thai Textiles', paper presented to The Asia Society, New York

LE MAY, R. 1926. *An Asian Arcady. The Land and Peoples of Northern Siam*, Cambridge; repr. 1986, White Lotus Co. Ltd, Bangkok

LING ROTH, H. 1918 (repr. 1977). *Studies in Primitive Looms*, Ruth Bean, Carlton, Bedford

McGILVRAY, D. 1912. *A half century among the Siamese and Lao*, Fleming H. Ravelle Co., London

NA NAKORN, P. 1979. 'Thai Costumes', *Holidays in Thailand*, Bangkok, pp. 36–45

NORTH EAST CROP DEVELOPMENT PROJECT, 1988. 'Report on the economics of sericulture by short term specialist in agricultural economics', Management Unit, North East Rainfed Agricultural Development Project, Tha Phra, Thailand

PEETATHAWATCHAI, V. 1973. *Esarn Cloth Design*, Faculty of Education, Khon Kaen University

PHISIT (PISIT), C. 1973. *Ban Chiang*, Rong Phikanet, Bangkok

PHISIT (PISIT), C., and GORMAN, C. 1976. 'Ban Chiang, a mosaic of impressions from the first two years', *Expedition* 18, 4

PISIT (PHISIT), C., and DISKUL, M.C. SUBHADRADIS. 1978. *Archaeologia Mundi, Thailand*, Nagel Publishers, Geneva

POTTER, SULAMITH HEINS, 1977. *Family life in a Northern Thai Village*, University of California Press, Berkeley

SAMOSORN, PAIROTE. 1989. *E-sarn Mural Paintings*, E-sarn Culture Center, Khon Kaen University and The Toyota Foundation, Japan

SANGAROON, KENOKPONGCHAI (ed.) 1986. *Wat Phumin and Wat Nong Bua*, Muang Boran Publishers, Bangkok

SATKUL, NANTA. 1970. *Dutch documents during the Ayuthya period 1572–1620 and 1620–1642 A.D.*, The Division of Fine Arts, Bangkok

S, A.M., and D N. 1927. *A Classified List of the Plants of Burma*, Rangoon Superintendent Government Printing and Stationery, Burma

SHAW, J. 1981. *Northern Thai Ceramics*, Oxford University Press, Kuala Lumpur

SHEARES, C. 1983. 'The ikat technique of textile patterning in Southeast Asia', *Heritage* 4, National Museum, Singapore, p. 33

SHEARES, C. 1984. 'Ikat Patterns from Kampuchea, Stylistic Influences', *Heritage* 7, National Museum, Singapore, pp. 45–53

SIMATRANG, SONE, 1983. *The Structure of Lanna Mural Paintings*, Vol. 2, Silpakorn University Press, Bangkok

SMITH, M. 1947. *A Physician at the Court of Siam*, Country Life Press, London

SUVATABANDHU, K. 1964. *Dye plants and Dyeing – A Handbook*, Brooklyn Botanic Garden Record (10th reprint, 1975)

SWEARER, D.K. 1974. 'Myth, legend and history in the Northern Thai Chronicles', *Journal of the Siam Society*, Vol. 62, Pt 1

TAMBIAH, S.J. 1970. *Buddhism and the Spirit Cults in North east Thailand*, Cambridge University Press

THAMAWAT, JERUWAN. 1980. *Poetry of the Lay People*, University of Maha Sarakham, Thailand

THE WORLD FELLOWSHIP OF BUDDHISTS, 1980. *Buddhism in Northern Thailand*, 13th conference, Thippanetr Publishing Co., Chiang Mai, Thailand

THE CENTRE FOR SOUTHEAST ASIAN STUDIES, 1985. *A Rice Growing Village Revisited. An integrated study of Rural Development in Northeast Thailand*, Kyoto University, Kyoto

VAN ESTERIK, P., and KRESS, N. 1978. 'An interpretation of Ban Chiang rollers: experiment and speculation', *Asian Perspectives*, 21

WARREN, W. 1970. *The Legendary American*, Houghton Mifflin Co., Boston

WHITE, J. 1982. *Ban Chiang. Discovery of a Lost Bronze Age*, University of Pennsylvania Press, Philadelphia

WIYADA, THONGMITR, 1983. *Wat Phra Sing*, Muang Boran Publishers, Bangkok

WONG, G. 1979. 'Tributary Trade between China and Southeast Asia in the Sung Dynasty', in *Chinese Celadons and Other Related Wares in Southeast Asia*, comp. Southeast Asia Ceramic Society, *Ars Orientalis*, Singapore

WOOD, W.A.R. 1933. *A History of Siam*, London

WRAY, E., ROSENFIELD, C., and BAILEY, D. 1972. *Ten Lives of the Buddha*, Weatherhill, New York and Tokyo

GLOSSARY

bencharongse   Five-coloured cloth of red, white, green, yellow and black.

Bun Kathin   Ceremony of merit-making held between the full moons of October and November.

Bun Phraawes   Ceremony of merit-making held after rice harvest.

charkha   Indian spinning-wheel.

chedi   Thai word for a religious mound containing relics of the Buddha. May also be called a *stupa*.

da moo   Northern Thai dialect for plied yarn.

dork   Thai word for flower.

dork chan   Thai word for sandalwood flower.

dork kaew   Thai word for white flower.

dork picun   Thai word for a small flower.

dta mok   Thai word to describe a supplementary warp used in weaving to produce a simple damask.

fuum kan   Reeds with teeth set close together.

fuum saa   Reeds with teeth set wide apart.

hau kathin   Thai word for a wooden palanquin used to bear gifts to the temple.

hoalaman   A mythical creature which features in the *Ramakien* (*Ramayana*) stories.

hom uan   Northern Thai word for a type of weaving pattern consisting of alternating thick- and thin-ply yarn arranged in bands in the warp and weft.

hua   Thai word for head.

ikat   Malay/Indonesian word for a resist-dye process in which yarns are tied in selected areas to prevent penetration of dye and to form patterns when the yarn is woven.

jaw   A large, flat, bamboo tray approximately 60 in (152 cm) in diameter with concentric compartments in which silkworms are placed to spin cocoons.

jok   Thai word for 'to pick' or 'lift out'. It describes a discontinuous supplementary-weft technique picked with the aid of a porcupine quill or using the fingers.

kathin   Presentation of gifts and robes to the monks.

kee krang   Red dye obtained from the resinous secretions of the insect *Lakshadia chinensis*.

kee lek   Thai word for a solution which is used to cleanse temple walls before painting.

khamin (*kamin*)   Thai word for turmeric, a yellow root vegetable used as a dye.

khanun   Tai word for jackfruit.

Khaw Phansa   The beginning of Buddhist Lent.

khit   Thai word to describe a continuous supplementary weft.

khram   Indigo paste.

khwan   Thai word for spirit.

kinnari   Female, semi-divine being whose upper half is human and lower half bird.

ko   Thai word to describe tapestry weave.

kon chook   Hair-cutting ceremony marking a child's entry to adult life.

kong   Device made of bamboo on which silk is wound after reeling.

kong toon   Thai word for dowry.

krang   Shellac used for red dye.

kuad khaw phi   Offering to a spirit, made on the advice of a spirit medium.

kut kreua   Stylised fern pattern used in weaving *jok*.

lakmee   A frame on which weft yarn is tensioned so that ties can be arranged in patterns.

Lao Nam Krang   A Tai ethnic sub-group from Phichit province, also called Lao Krang.

lei sin kyo   Burmese weaving pattern meaning 'four stripes'.

lungyi   Burmese word for a man's loincloth and a woman's skirt.

luntaya   A type of Burmese weaving pattern.

maha kyo shwei taik   Burmese weaving pattern meaning 'great line golden building'.

mai   Thai word for wood.

makham   Thai word for tamarind.

makrut   A type of crinkled lime, *Citrus hystrix*, used in certain dye recipes to achieve a level of acidity.

matmi   Thai term to describe resist-dye patterns made by tying groups of yarn in selected areas to prevent dye penetration. Known also as ikat.

ma tum   Thai word for seedpods of *Aegle marmelos* which are used in the preparation of yellow dye.

maun   Thai word for a pillow or cushion.

muang   Tai word for a city-state.

muk   Thai word for supplementary-warp technique, also called *khit*.

naga   A mythical serpent capable of assuming human form.

nam krang   Thai term for a red dye bath made from the resinous secretions of the insect *Lakshadia chinensis*.

nam tan ta nod   A solution of lime, fine sand and sugar used to coat temple walls in preparation for mural painting.

nok gatap   Thai word for pigeon.

nok kapbua   Thai word for heron.

nok ring   Thai word for vulture.

Org Phansa   The end of Buddhist Lent.

pa nung   See *pha chong kaben*.

paso   Burmese male costume.

patola   Indian double-ikat textile; both warp and weft are tie-dyed.

payar   Isan courting prose.

pha   Thai word for cloth.

pha biang   A rectangular woven textile worn around the shoulders or across the chest. In northern Thailand it is called a *pha sabai*.

pha chet   Ceremonial shoulder textile worn by Tai Lue men.

pha chet noi   A small woven textile used to wipe the mouth.

pha chong kaben   A rectangular textile wrapped around the waist, passed between the legs and tucked in at the back, or front, to form a pantaloon. It is also called a *pha toi*.

pha hang   A rectangular textile wrapped around the waist and drawn between the legs to create a kind of pantaloon. It is worn in novice processions and used as a coffin cover.

pha hawi haw   A set of silk clothes presented to the bridegroom by the parents of the bride.

pha hom   Thai word for blanket.

pha hom uan   Northern Thai dialect for a type of weaving pattern.

pha koma   A rectangular textile used as a sash, turban, bathing wrap or as a cradle for a baby.

phak hom   A plant, similar to spinach, used in a recipe for finishing cloth.

phakhwan   Cone-shaped dish offered to the spirits during marriage ceremonies.

pha lop   Bed sheet.

pha nung   See *pha chong kaben*.

pha prae wa   A shoulder-sash worn by Phu Tai women.

pha sabai   A rectangular textile worn over the shoulder or across the chest. In north-east Thailand it is called a *pha biang*.

pha sarong   A rectangular textile 2–3 yds (1.8–2.7 m) long worn by men, sewn with one side seam to create a tubular garment tucked at the waist with a pleat. Also called a sarong.

phasin (pha sin)   A woman's woven tubular skirt with one or two side seams.

pha toi   See *pha chong kaben*.

pha tung   A temple banner.

Phu Tai   Tai ethnic sub-group living in north-east Thailand, mainly in Kalasin, Ubon and Mukdahan.

pla buk   A species of fish.

pla kaow   A species of fish.

pla sua   A species of fish.

prae sapai   Thai word for a silk chiffon shoulder-sash.

rachasee   The legendary Thai king of animals, born of two bears.

rai   Measurement of land: 1 *rai* = 0.16 ha.

sala   A meeting-house.

sarong   Man's tubular loincloth.

sellac   A red-brown dye.

sin   Central panel of a woman's *phasin* skirt.

sinsawt   Wedding gift from the groom's parents to the bride's parents.

suea   Thai for shirt or blouse.

Tai   An ethnic group, made up of several sub-groups, speaking Tai languages and dialects. The Tai inhabit an area from Assam through Burma, Thailand, Laos and Vietnam and parts of southern China.

Tai Lao   Tai ethnic group from Laos.

Tai Lue   Tai ethnic group from Sipsong Panna, China. Many are now settled in Nan province, north Thailand.

Tai Phuan   Tai Lao group from Xieng Khouang province, Laos.

Tai Yai   Tai from the Shan states of Burma.

Tai Yuan   Tai ethnic group living in Lanna.

teen   Hem border of a woman's *phasin*.

teen jok   Hem border of a woman's *phasin* woven with a discontinuous supplementary weft.

Thai   Citizen of Thailand.

thepanum   Thai word for a worshipping deity.

tieo sado   Thai word for wide-legged indigo trousers.

wat   Thai Buddhist monastery complex.

INDEX

PHOTOGRAPHIC ACKNOWLEDGEMENTS

The author and publishers are grateful to the following for permission to reproduce photographs:

Gill Boardman 132–3; Addison Castle 84, 85; Isan Culture Museum, Khon Kaen University 2–3, 74, 76–7, 87, 108–9, 129, 130; Pitt Rivers Museum, Oxford 34 *top*, 100 *top*, 101, 107; Kim Retka 121 *top*; Siam Society 24, 26, 34 *bottom*, 100 *bottom*, 114, 131; Smithsonian Institution, Washington, DC 43 *bottom*, 122.

The maps on pages 16, 23 and 27 are by Technical Art Services.